The Compacted

Book of

World War 1

Fascinating First World War Stories

Plus 200 Trivia Questions

for Your Trivia Domination

History Compacted

ISBN: 9798672917573

Table of Contents

A Note

From History Compacted

Hi there!

This is Jason Chen, founder of History Compacted. Before you continue your journey to the past, I want to take a quick moment to explain our position on history and the purpose of our books.

To us, history is more than just facts, dates, and names. We see history as pieces of stories that led to the world we know today. Besides, it makes it much more fun seeing it that way too.

That is why History Compacted was created: to tell amazing stories of the past and hopefully inspire you to search for more. After all, history would be too big for any one book. But what each book can give you is a piece of the puzzle to help you get to that fuller picture.

Lastly, I want to acknowledge the fact that history is often told from different perspectives. Depending on the topic and your upbringing, you might agree or disagree with how we present the facts. I understand disagreements are inevitable. That is why, with a team of diverse writers, we aim to tell each story from a more neutral perspective. I hope this note can help you better understand our position and goals.

Now without further ado, let your journey to the past begin!

Introduction

In 1908, Austria-Hungary annexed Bosnia-Herzegovina, a lush land to its south that had once been ruled by the Ottoman Empire. This move had been controversial both among the court of the Austro-Hungarian Empire and with the Serbian government. The Serbian government and people of this tiny Balkan nation felt that Bosnia-Herzegovina should be theirs as they had more in common with its populace.

Archduke Franz Ferdinand, the heir apparent and inspector general of the empire's army, had been one of the most vocal with his opposition. He had no love for the Serbians. In fact, Ferdinand often called them "pigs" and "thieves," among other more colorful names. However, the archduke knew that taking this land would lead to more political unrest in the volatile Balkan regions. Still, he had a job to do, and setting his opposition aside, agreed to the task sent down from his Uncle Franz Josef, the emperor. He would travel to Sarajevo in the summer of 1914 to inspect military exercises and ensure the troops were ready for combat. This decision would turn fatal and launch a series of events that ignited hostilities and a war to end all wars.

The news of the archduke's impending visit traveled quickly. Nationalism had been rising in Serbia and Bosnia-Herzegovina ever since the empire had annexed the nation. Among these nationalist and revolutionary associations was a group known as the Young Bosnians. Upon hearing of the archduke's plans, this group of radicals knew it was time to let the Austrians see the country was theirs.

So, they sat down and began plotting to assassinate the archduke. Three of the students, Gavrilo Princip, Trifko Grabež, and Nedeljko Čabrinović, would be tasked with procuring the weapons and training needed to execute the plan.

In May, these young men made their way across the Serbian border to the capital city of Belgrade. They were to meet with a group known as the Black Hand, one of Serbia's prominent liberation groups. The Black Hand was tied to the Serbian Army, so they had access to a wide variety of weapons that would be helpful in the execution of the assassination.

They delivered multiple hand bombs, pistols, and cyanide pills (to be taken if they were caught) into the hands of these Bosnian revolutionaries. For days after, the delivery shots rang out in Belgrade Park as Princip, Grabež, and Čabrinović practiced their pistol skills. When confident that they had the knowledge and skill level needed to be successful, the trio made their way back over the border with the assistance of the Black Hand.

Ignoring concerns and warnings over terrorist activity and potential danger, the archduke, accompanied by his wife, Sophie, set out from their estate on the warm summer morning of June 23. Not long into the drive, the driver and the royals began to smell something burning. They pulled to the side of the road, and jumping from the car, they found that the car axles had gotten a little hotter than was recommended and were on fire. The archduke commented, as the couple and their guards waited for the car to cool down, that this may not have been the most auspicious start to the trip. Once the minor detour was finished, the couple continued on their way, finally making it to the small resort town outside of Sarajevo that would be their home for the next week.

While Ferdinand walked lines of troops and reviewed battle strategies, Sophie took the time to tour schools and orphanages in and around the small city. Tired of the monotony of the day and the small town they were staying in, the couple made the bold move of driving into Sarajevo to stroll through the famous markets. Walking through the markets attracted some attention. Large crowds of Bosnians quickly formed, including one of the men determined to end the rule of Austria-Hungary over the nation, Gavrilo Princip.

Despite the rising hatred amongst the citizens, the crowd that gathered to watch the archduke and archduchess ramble through the markets was welcoming and polite. After this tour, the couple was scheduled to attend a banquet held by religious and political leaders, which would leave the couple with one day left in Sarajevo.

After spending the morning taking care of errands and writing to his loved ones, Archduke Ferdinand and Sophie jumped on a train bound for Sarajevo and their last day of festivities. Ferdinand would walk side by side with Sophie, an unusual occurrence for the archduchess, to conduct the last inspection of their trip before they would begin their motorcade toward the city hall. The first car carried four police officers while the royal visitors were housed in the second car, followed by a third with more security. The streets were lined with welcoming crowds, and it seemed safe enough, so

Ferdinand decided it would be best to ride with their car's top down.

This would allow the couple to greet their loyal and loving subjects as they drove down the avenues. The choice to ride with their top down, however, would be a deadly mistake, for spread out amongst those adoring crowds were seven men, all members of the Young Bosnians. Security for the Austro-Hungarian conclave had been less critical than meals and political meetings, and so the archduke's route had been published ahead of the procession in order to ensure there were adoring crowds to meet them. So as the line of cars made its way down the Appel Quay, the freedom fighters took their places.

The cars passed one of the perpetrators, but the fear got the best of him, and he did not act. The vehicles moved further down the road and passed yet another, and he too lost his nerve. But as the caravan continued, the next young man and one of the three sent to Belgrade in May, Nedeljko Čabrinović, would shore his courage up and make his move. Working his way through the crowd, he arrived near the front. He watched as the motorcade approached, and leaning over to a fellow spectator, quietly asked which car was the archduke's.

The spectator, thinking nothing of the question, motioned toward the second car. As the vehicle passed by the central police station, Čabrinović pulled the pin on one of the hand bombs that the Black Hand had given him and lobbed it toward the archduke's vehicle.

Out of the corner of his eye, the driver saw something substantial being thrown at the car and accelerated. The bomb, instead of landing in the vehicle, hit the rolled-up roof and rolled backward, falling under the vehicle behind the couple. The explosion rocked the motorcade, and the crowd lined up to watch the royals as they made their way to the center of town. Several people in the crowd were injured along with two officers, but the attack had failed to affect the intended target.

Seeing that he had failed, Čabrinović pushed his way through the panicking people and jumped into the riverbed opposite the police station. While reaching for the cyanide pill in an attempt to kill himself, he was apprehended.

As he was led away in cuffs, all he would say was, "I am a Serbian hero!"

Rattled but not deterred, the archduke and his wife pressed on toward the event scheduled at the city hall. After the state event was over, the archduke and his wife demanded to visit the wounded from the earlier attack. Knowing this could be another opportunity for the dissidents to attack, the security team rushed the two into their vehicle and sped through the streets toward the hospital. As the motorcade rushed down the street, the first car turned down a small lane. Unfortunately, they had chosen the wrong road. And as the cars began to back up, the man standing in the alley, Gavrilo Princip, took the opportunity to finish the mission.

The slender young man stepped forward and drew his pistol. Two shots rang out, and the security of the royal couple sprang into action. However, it was too late. The two shots had been at close range and struck Ferdinand and Sophie. Both now lay bleeding in the cabin of their vehicle as their men tried to restrain the assailant and save their leader and his wife.

Ferdinand was hit in the neck and Sophie in the stomach. As they lay there, bleeding out, Ferdinand pled with Sophie to survive if only for their children. Alas, it was not to be as it took mere minutes before the archduke and his beloved wife lay dead.

Princip, too young for the death penalty, would admit to killing the archduke but expressed remorse about the archduchess. He would be sentenced to 20 years and die in jail before the war that he helped start would come to its conclusion.

Chapter One

A Turbulent World

World War I was a war such as the world had never seen. New technology and warfare tactics would be introduced. New alliances and rivalries would form, and the world would never be the same again. But there were already catalysts present before the first shots had even been fired.

Europe and the world had been changing, and this set the stage for the turbulent atmosphere of the time. Everything, from the final death throes of imperialism to a surge in nationalism, all contributed to the volatile state of affairs in Europe. This ever-changing world also played a role in the industrialization of war, which brought with it a wave of militarism. It seemed that Europe was a ticking time bomb.

The assassination simply was the last straw in a series of events that would finally collapse that delicate balance.

Franco-Prussian War

Many wars had been fought over the previous century, and each played a part in setting the stage for a Europe on the brink. The most recent conflict and perhaps the one that played the biggest role in prepping for the coming World War was the Franco-Prussian War. The impact that this war had on the geography of Europe would further the already-tense relationship between France and the German states. With the conclusion of the war in 1871, the newly-formed Germany would emerge a confident and robust powerhouse in the European landscape.

The Treaty of Frankfurt would eventually end the war. This agreement would cede almost all of the Alsace and a good chunk of the Lorraine to the Germans. The loss of land and the French Army's devastating defeat added to the age-old rivalry between the French and the Germans and made sure that the tension between these two peoples would live on for decades to come. In fact, over the next 40 years, those tensions would build, and when the conflict in the East began to take shape, the two bitter enemies had all the reasons in the world to take up arms against each other once again.

Alliances

Even though most of the ruling houses of Europe were related, the alliances were not formed from these relationships. Instead, it was through the imperialistic expansion during the hundreds of years leading to the 20th century and the consecutive wars previously fought that crafted the alliances. These alliances would be a critical factor in the break out of the Great War. Russia was allied to both Serbia and France while Germany was allied to Austria-Hungary. The British and the French had also signed a mutual defense agreement. The tangled web of backroom alliances and political unrest was kindling to an already smoldering fire.

In the 1880s, following the Franco-Prussian War, the Russians and Germans had developed a beneficial alliance, but with Bismarck losing grace and being removed, this relationship was lost. The new German government focused more on their relations with nations in the Mediterranean, figuring there was too much difference between Tsarist Russia and the French Republic for them to worry about the two countries teaming up. Still scathing from the defeat and land lost in the Franco-Prussian War, the French saw an opportunity, and the Franco-Russian alliance was born.

The French had ample money and a decent military to offer, and the Russians have military resources. Afraid that the new and more powerful German state would attack, the French knew they needed to build an alliance with the only other strategic force that could stand up to the Germans. After years of negotiations in 1894, the two nations signed a treaty. The agreement stated that if Germany or Italy with German assistance attacked France, the Russians would send troops. On the other hand, if Germany or Austria with German assistance attacked Russia, the French would do the same.

Another alliance that would play a part in the opening shots of the war was the Russo-Serbian alliance. Early in the 19th century, Serbians had begun to fight harder for their independence from the Ottoman Empire. The Russians still had an ax to grind with the Ottomans as they sided with France in the Napoleonic wars against Russia. So, when the political and nationalist uprising began, the Russians looked to give aid and ally themselves with the Serbs.

In the alliance of 1807, the Russians offered assistance to the Serbian rebels. Rather than live autonomously under the

Ottoman rule, the Serbians took the deal. So, when Austria-Hungary declared war on Serbia after the archduke's assassination, the Russians, per the agreement, had no choice but to move to the borders to lend aid to their allies.

The entente cordiale was yet another alliance that left its mark on the world and ushered in another nation into the battle. In the early part of the 20th century, the British and French were still imperialistic powers, and this caused friction between the two nations. In order to calm the disputes in North Africa and other colonies, the two countries sat down and hammered out an agreement of mutual defense. The contract stated that Egypt would defend Britain, and Morocco would defend France. But for France, there was more involved. In fact, much like its agreement with Russia, there were safety measures in the treaty to help protect them if the ever-growing German military felt it necessary to attack France.

The last alliance that played a part at the beginning of the war was the Triple Alliance. This alliance was the mutual defense agreement between Austria-Hungary, Germany, and Italy. This treaty, like the other agreements, promised military support if the nations were attacked by France or Russia (or any of those two nations' allies).

With defense agreements in place, the battle lines were drawn, and the war would begin. On one side you would have the Central Powers (this included Germany, Bulgaria, Austria-Hungary, and the Ottoman Empire) and on the other hand the Allied Forces (this included England, France, Russia, Japan, the U.S., Romania, as well as later in the war, Italy).

Because of these alliances and ramifications of the political environment of the time, the war would be fought on two sides, dividing Europe into the western and eastern fronts and last from 1914-1918. Within these four years, over 16 million soldiers and civilians would lose their lives. This level of carnage had never been experienced, and thanks to the use of modern warfare techniques (like trench warfare) and new devastating weapons, it would become the norm in all future wars.

Chapter Two

The Eastern Front

The Austro-Hungarian Empire, shocked by the assassination of Archduke Ferdinand and his wife, knew that the aggression of the Serbian Nationalists wouldn't end there. So, the leaders of the empire gathered and decided that the only way to curb this would be to invade the small Balkan nation. But first, they would need to reach out to their friends—the Germans—and make sure that if they did that, they would hold up their end of the alliance.

Assured that Germany had their back, the Austro-Hungarian king and leaders drafted a very stern and precise ultimatum. This document was rushed to the Serbian capital in late July. There were many edicts laid out in the papers of that ultimatum, including the suppression of anti-Austrian media and the right of Austrian officials to man their own investigation into the assassination. Serbia would agree to all but one of the edicts—the independent investigation of the archduke's murder—and for the Austrians, this was enough to void the entire pact.

Feeling that this was an acknowledgment of their cooperation in the incident, the Austrians cut off all diplomatic avenues with the Serbian government and began to prepare for war. The Serbians had feared this would be the reaction, so before handing down their answer to their mighty neighbor to the north, they had sent word to their allies, the Russians, for help.

Not only did the Russians see this as an obligation, but they were also looking at the potential of gaining traction in the Balkans and the Black Sea coastal areas. So, the Russians began mobilizing their army in support of their Serbian allies. This alliance would turn this part of the conflict into a Russian/Austria-Hungary battle, just like the western front was a Franco-German war. With the battle lines drawn on July 28, 1914, just a month after the assassination of the archduke, Austria-Hungary declared war on Serbia and effectively began the Great War.

Though most associate World War I with the battles of the western front, it was the eastern front where the entire conflict began. While the world's eyes were on the newly created trench warfare of the western front and its horrors, significant battles and maneuvers were being carried out on the other side of Europe. The war on this front was not a war fought with new technology and techniques; instead, it was fought with the tried and true methods of previous wars.

For Russia, like Germany, this war would be fought on two fronts. The empire's alliance with France would force it to not only send troops to fight the Austro-Hungarians in the Balkans but also the German Army as well in East Prussia. This eastern front would be fought over a 310-mile stretch of land that ran from the Baltic Sea in the north to the Romanian border in the south. The fighting would see the Russians sending a million troops to the front to start, and throughout the four-year war, that number would jump to over three million. Though this part of the war did not see as much press in the western countries, there were still battles that would play a vital role in the length and culmination of the war.

Battle of Tannenberg (August 1914)

The eastern front began with a flurry of skirmishes that showed the vast differences between not only the equipment but also the sheer numbers of the German, Russian, and Austro-Hungarian Armies. Both Germany and Austria-Hungary, as well as their adversaries, the Russian, had greater distances to move than those fighting on the western front, and this led the Germans to decide to leave just one army cohort to protect the East Prussian border. The distances would also play a part in keeping this theater of the Great War more traditional in its tactics and movements. In the end, Tannenberg would be a devastating loss for the Russians. Through logistical and strategic miscalculations, the Russian Army would be crushed in just over a week.

With their French allies in the west feeling the pressure of the onslaught of German military movements, the Russian commander-in-chief, Grand Duke Nicholas, answered their call and began preparations for a significant military move against the Germans. The grand duke, feeling that the sheer number of Russian troops would be enough to pull German forces from the western battles, deployed his first and second armies to East Prussia. However, though they were many, the units were not fully prepared to engage in the intense battles ahead. The grand duke had signed off on the plan to mobilize his troops into action too early, but the fault for the ultimate defeat at Tannenberg fell squarely on General Yakov Zhilinsky.

Zhilinsky had held the position of chief of the general staff for several years and would keep his job during the first few months of the war until the mistakes and miscalculations of the Battle of Tannenberg would come to light. When the war broke out, France called on their Russian allies to help with the fight, and Zhilinsky answered that call with a promise to mobilize 800,000 men within the first two weeks of the war.

The Russian forces were not ready for this expenditure of men and equipment, and so there was a lot of pressure on not only the troops but also the military leadership. This promise would cause the Russian leadership to make some very rash decisions. Overextending and over-promising were the biggest of those. Not only had Zhilinsky promised an excessive amount of men, but he had also promised the French that he would attack both the Germans and the Austro-Hungarians simultaneously, and this stretched his resources very thin. For the Prussian campaign of his military mobilization, Zhilinsky chose to use two of his armies, the First Army led by General

Rennenkampf and the Second Army led by General Samsonov.

The plan was simple. The First Army would move into East Prussia from the east, which Zhilinsky felt would cause the German Army to move defensive forces from the French line to shore up the woefully inadequate troop count stationed there. Then two days later, the Second Army would move up from the south and attack the German forces from the rear, cutting access off to Vistula River (in what is today's Poland), which would give the Russians control over a significant transport lane. The plan on paper was a solid one and one that caused the Germans to spring to action quickly once the news of the impending attack was relayed to command.

However, where this strategic plan failed was in the execution. On top of poor leadership and the Russian Army's lack of readiness, two logistical miscalculations led to the utter devastation of the Second Russian Army.

The first of the logistical oversights was the distance and geography that separated the two armies. In between the two armies were the Masurian Lakes. The lakes stretched over 50 miles, and that, coupled with Königsberg, a highly fortified area, would hinder a rapid advancement from the south by

26

Samsonov's men. This geography would narrow the route to just 40 miles and would limit Rennenkampf's ability to advance as fast as they would need to meet Samsonov's army from the south. Unfortunately for the Russians, the Germans knew this and would use it to their advantage in the coming battle. The second issue was one that was more of a problem for Samsonov's troops. In preparation to paralyze the German forces and keep them from invading Russian territory, the military divisions before them had desolated the railways and destroyed roads, which though was intended to hinder the German advancement, made it difficult for their own troop movements as well.

On August 17, Rennenkampf's First Army would begin their push into East Prussia. The troops moved in a flurry against Germany's Eighth Army commanded by General Max von Prittwitz. The battle was furious, but eventually, the larger Russian forces, despite their inadequate training, were able to push back multiple German divisions of infantry and cavalry. The first battle waged on for three days, and by the time that it had come to a decisive conclusion, Samsonov's Second Army was able to get into position for the next phase of the battle. However, due to the hurried pace, Samsonov's men were tired and hungry; not all the supplies had been able to make it, nor had the entire cohort, which left them at a disadvantage.

Unfortunately for Samsonov, his troop's movement and their location were spotted. On August 20, Prittwitz received word that the Russian Second Army was approaching from the rear and that the numbers were significantly more than the army to the north. These revelations seemed to worry General Prittwitz, the man in charge of the Eighth Army, and so he sought council with several of his most regarded subordinates.

In this meeting, he expressed concern that the Russian force moving from the south would cut off any route of escape and put forth a plan to take his troops and set up behind the Vistula River. Despite the strong opposition to this plan from both General Grünert and Lieutenant Colonel Hoffman, the general still felt his way was the best. Though eventually, he would be convinced that his strategy was too risky and move on to another option.

An offensive would be launched on Samsonov's western flank. In preparation for this maneuver, Prittwitz moved three divisions from the north and integrated them with the soldiers of the XX Corps. Then the general would have the rest of the northern troops retreat to the west. With the troop movements, the Eighth Army's headquarters moved to Mülhausen. The maneuvers executed, Prittwitz soon received word that his men had been able to break away from the advancement of

Rennenkampf's forces and that the tactics had stalled the movement of Samsonov's troops. But that wouldn't be the only piece of news relayed to the general. His inaction and insistence on retreating to Vistula to hold the line there had alarmed the German leadership back in Berlin. Realizing that the eastern front of the battle was going to be just as tricky as the western front, they had decided to replace Prittwitz with proven leadership. A train was on its way, and on it was the division's new leader, General Paul von Hindenburg (future President of Germany), and his chief of staff, Erich Ludendorff.

Ludendorff and Lieutenant Colonel Hoffman (one of Prittwitz's former advisors) corresponded back and forth and would join together to create a plan. They would form this plan using Hoffman's experience and knowledge of the Russian Army, which he had gained while observing the Japanese during the Russo-Japanese War. The plan would decimate Samsonov's troops. The tacticians would attack Samsonov's left flank again this time with the power of six different divisions. The first step was to send for reinforcements from the north as the number of soldiers currently available to the Germans was less than the Russians of the Second Army.

Calling for these reinforcements was a gamble, as it left just a cavalry front to hold the defensive line against Rennenkampf, who was still advancing near Gumbinnen. The reinforcements would sweep up from Samsonov's right while the already-present troops would advance on his left. The two German forces would push through, surrounding the center of the Russian cohort and blocking Samsonov from moving on his target.

These were risky maneuvers as they entailed large troop movements to go unnoticed by the enemy. However, the lack of communication between the two Russian generals and the German's ability to decipher the wireless orders sent by Samsonov to his troops made the German troop movements very easy to keep hidden.

After several tactical victories over Samsonov's flanks, the Second Army's core was cut off from any means of escape. The Russian troops became a hungry mass of untrained soldiers, and despite efforts to push through, they realized that the end was near. To protect his troops and himself, Samsonov ordered the remainder of his forces to turn south. Knowing that the roads would be watched and patrolled by the German forces, he urged his troops into the woods, and without knowledge of the area and with very little hope, his cohort would end up lost in the dense forests.

The general, painfully aware that all was lost, strolled, unbeknownst to his advisors, into the woods on the morning of August 30. Amid the frustration and fear in the camp, a shot rang out. The general had taken his own life instead of dealing with the shame and potential capture by the German forces. And with that one bullet, the Battle of Tannenberg came to an end.

Gallipoli Campaign (February 1915-January 1916)

The Dardanelles Campaign, also known as the Gallipoli Campaign, was a British and French operation in Turkey. After the Russian leaders appealed to their allies—the French—and, in turn, the British, for help, the two Allied Forces banded together and set out for the Aegean Sea. The two forces hoped they could occupy Constantinople and gain control of the straits that joined the Black Sea with the Aegean. The occupation of the straits and Constantinople would cut off the Ottoman Empire from the Caucuses and ease the stress on the Russian forces. A victory would be a pivotal part of removing the Ottoman Empire from the war altogether, thereby weakening the Germans and Austro-Hungarians' position and leading to the end of the conflict. Unfortunately, the campaign would be riddled with miscalculations and underestimations.

Between 1904 and 1911, the British had toyed with the idea of moving on the Ottoman Empire to gain further control in the Middle East. Once the idea was examined closer, it was deemed likely to be a devastating defeat and was put on the back burner. Yet, when war broke out in 1914 and the Turkish allied themselves with the Austro-Hungarian Empire, the British and their allies—the French, felt it was worth retaking a look at this proposal. So, when Grand Duke Nicholas asked for help in January of 1915, the British took the opportunity not only to settle their interests in the region but also to help their Russian allies by cutting off the Turkish insurgence into the Caucasus front. When the British decided to help the grand duke, they knew that the Dardanelles was the place to execute this maneuver. They also knew that it would take a massive collaboration between both the main military forces and the British naval fleet.

Led by then First Lord of the Admiralty, Winston Churchill, the British command decided to run a solely naval driven operation at first. Not wanting to use their best ships as they were needed in the North Sea to hold the barricade there, the British decided to use warships that were too old to be in commission. The use of old ships would protect their endeavors in the North Sea, and if the campaign failed, there would be minimal loss of money and useful ships. However, that plan was short-lived as it soon became very evident that there would also have to be ground attacks. The shores of the Dardanelles would have to be taken and held so that the fleet could do its job. So, with this decision firmly in play, a British military presence began building in Egypt along with a small contingent from their French allies to aid their seafaring brothers in arms.

On February 19, the initial battle was set to begin, but the weather would not permit it, and so the operation was halted. After six days of inclement weather, the skies cleared, and the mission could move forward. Marines landed, accompanied by combat engineers set for demolition duties on the beaches without any opposition. Still, the weather turned quickly, and this portion of the mission would stall just like the initial launch. It wasn't until March 18 that the actual barrage of bombs began in preparation for the fleet to make their move. After several hours of bombardment, the British had lost three ships, and several more were damaged. The loss of these ships was a clear sign; this mission was going to need more than the might of the fleet.

After regrouping and restructuring their plan, the mission continued in late April. This time, troop transports amassed on the island of Lemnos with the intention of landing in two pivotal places along the Gallipoli peninsula. On April 25, the British forces would land at Cape Helles, and the ANZAC (Australian and New Zealand forces) would take the other beachhead. As the battle progressed, the Allied armies moved forward, securing small beachheads along the way. However, these victories were small and difficult to obtain as the insurgents were met with Turkish resistance, led by the man who would later be known as Atatürk, Mustafa Kemal.

The British forces struggled to gain land and needed to find a strategic tipping point for their next landings. Three months later, on August 6, another wave of soldiers landed at Suvla Bay. The Turkish had moved troops from this location as they felt the British would never attack it (though one commander, Mustafa Kemal, warned that this would be the location but was dismissed) because it was a naturally fortified region. So, the Turkish leadership had left a bare-bones presence. Even with the limited troop resources, the Turkish forces were able to stop the invading forces in their tracks eventually, thanks to their knowledge of the landscape and the natural fortification of the bay. With all the unsuccessful pushes and attempts to take the Dardanelles, the British felt it was time to replace their leader, and in September, would do just that. However, it was too little too late.

By late November, it was evident that the campaign would not be a victory for the British and French forces, and in waves, the Allied Forces left the shores of Turkey. By the first week of January 1916, all troops had been evacuated. The British's bid to take the straits and help the Russians had failed, and dealt the British a devastating defeat.

Brusilov Offensive (June-September 1916)

In February of 1916, the Battle of Verdun began on the western front. In response to this, the French called on their allies to help them out. By having the British and the Russians attack different fronts, the French hoped that a chunk of the German forces would move to shore up the holes that these offensives would open up. This tactic had worked in previous instances, so why not try it again? Both the British and the Russians agreed. This agreement would lead to several battles, including the Battle of Somme on the western front and the Battle of Vilna and the Brusilov Offensive on the eastern front.

The Russians initially attacked at Lake Narocz in Belarus. That campaign did not end well for the Russian Army. The Russians would begin this conflict with a barrage of artillery attacks. Unfortunately for them, they were inaccurate and would do little damage to the German artillery. The Russian troops, once the artillery had finished, would cross No Man's Land between the two armies in groups instead of spreading out. This miscalculation would make these troops easy targets for the still intact German artillery. The poor artillery execution would lead to a demoralizing defeat for the Russians and require them to regroup and try again. So, with that defeat, the Russian military began to plan a diversionary tactic near Vilna, which is now part of Poland. This battle was a disaster as well, and the Russians desperately needed a battle that would hold up their end of the bargain.

While these attacks were being executed and done so poorly, there was a Russian force sitting in the southwest part of the eastern front. This force was commanded by the highly experienced general named Alexei Brusilov. He and his troops sat, with no plans from the big brass coming down for them to do anything other than holding the line and keep the Austro-Hungarian forces from moving into Ukraine.

The elderly general knew him, and his extremely well-prepared troops could be of more use, so he sent word to the Russian military leaders asking if he could have permission to make a move. His troops were recovered from their previous victories, he had plenty of supplies, and he believed his men could handle the campaign. Many of the generals back in the capitol felt that this maneuver would end up being the same disaster as the others had been, but Brusilov pushed them harder, knowing he could be successful.

The brass finally agreed but didn't expect very much from this offensive, but they would be proven very wrong. Brusilov took the time to train his troops using full-sized replicas of the intended targets. This training allowed his men to calculate with precision where to aim their artillery. He used air reconnaissance to gain knowledge of these locations' layouts and defenses and kept this all under tight wraps until his troops were ready to execute the offensive. Starting the assault on June 4, in the city of Lutsk, Brusilov and his troops laid siege to the Austro-Hungarian Fourth Army lead by the Prince of the Habsburg Dynasty, Archduke Joseph Ferdinand. Shocked at the precision and brutality of the Russian attack, the Austrian line was demolished on the first day of the offensive.

Over the next two days, Brusilov led his men through Lutsk, devastated the Austrian troops, and gained 50 miles of territory. Once the Austrian forces were on the brink, the units of Slavic soldiers deserted them, leaving them to the mercy of the Russian troops. The first battle was successful, and

Brusilov would push on in the hopes of making even more gains for his beloved Russia. This well-executed push led to over 130,000 casualties and the capture of 200,000 prisoners. The Battle of Lutsk was just the beginning of his march, and over the next several months, he continued to devastate the southwestern line of the eastern front.

The offensive would be carried out along about a 200-mile stretch of the front that started from the Pripet Marshes down to the Carpathian Mountains of Romania. With nearly 2,000 guns, Brusilov's men pushed forward even though the numbers favored the Austro-Hungarian forces. However, with the rapid-fire onslaught, the Russian troops overwhelmed the Austrian line, perhaps because the Austrian forces underestimated the Russians' preparedness. Once the Austrians were pushed back to the Carpathians, they realized that they had underestimated the Russian forces and had lost too many supplies and men, so they reached out to their allies for reinforcements.

Eventually, in September, the push had exhausted Brusilov's supplies, and with no further help coming, the offensive had to come to an end. But by the time the offensive had ended, Brusilov and his men had captured approximately 400,000 men and 10,000 square miles of land. The push had tarnished the Habsburg's reputation as well as the military career of the prince. Along with that, two other military campaigns had felt the repercussions of this unexpected attack. Austrian military forces had to pull back from efforts to take the Trentino region of Italy, and the western front had several German divisions rerouted to help reinforce their allies, which, in the end, may have cost the Germans the Battle of Verdun.

Battle of Mărășești (July-September 1917)

The Romanians had entered the war in 1916, and immediately became a focus of the eastern front. One of the last and main battles of the Romanian campaign was the Battle of Mărășești. By the spring of 1917, the eastern front and the Russian military had been driven into chaos and disarray. With issues at home, the Russians had become unfocused, and the Allied Forces on the eastern front had experienced a series of devastating losses. In the hopes of turning the tides back in their favor on the Romanian front, the Russians (what was left of them) and the Romanian forces began to make plans for a two-pronged plan that would push the Austrians out of Romanian territory permanently. The first attack would be on the area surrounding Nămoloasa, and then once the damage had been done there, the combined forces would attack the Germans and Austrian troops in and near Mărășești.

39

However, before they could launch the first attack, it was abandoned, and the troops meant for that battle were relocated to be support for the Battle of Mărăşeşti. The forces of the two adversaries were pretty evenly matched; however, the Romanians, being strategic, had shored up sections along the attack route with extra troops, which would benefit them strategically in the long run and swing the needle in their direction. The attack then started with two days of heavy artillery on the German and Austrian positions aided by well-scouted aerial reconnaissance.

The ground offensive would begin with the Romanian Second Army flanked by the Russian Ninth and Seventh Armies going up against the Austro-Hungarian First Army. Still, with the two days of intense bombardment, this force had been shocked and was a little unsure of what was happening. Phase one of the battle would lead to Romanians taking the Teiuş hill in the village of Mărăşeşti. In the early morning of July 24, the two divisions would flank the forces and clear the path, eventually leading to them holding the Încărcătoarea clearing.

The second phase would start simultaneously with the previous maneuvering and the Fourth Romanian Army Corps pushing left across the land toward the Coada Văii - Babei clearing. At the same time, in the southern portion of the battlefield, the Romanian Second Army would be moving toward the same clearing, then the front line would begin moving to the hills north of Lepşa. Here, the Romanians felt they had an advantage over their enemies as they were used to fighting in this rugged and uneven terrain.

The German and Austrian forces were warned about these plans but felt that they could easily defend themselves and eventually land their own counter-attack that would halt the Romanian Armies' march. Unfortunately, the Romanians' familiarity with the land and love for their homeland would dash the German/Austrian forces' hopes.

The Austro-Hungarians and Germans planned to rely on their defensive lines and preparations to halt the Romanian advancement. These defenses came in two different forms, which had been used to much success in other parts of the war. The first was structures they called resistance centers. These were a series of trenches that were connected and covered by artillery. At crucial junctures, these trench systems would be topped with a steel dome and other military implementations to help form a shelter. In these junctures, troops or munitions would be stored, and these enclosures were intended to help keep them safe as well as give the troops housed in them a tactical advantage.

The other aspect of their defensive line was trenches. Hurriedly crafted over the last few weeks, the trenches that had been dug were remarkably well-crafted. Though the trenches were executed masterfully, the two defensive techniques could not match up to the knowledge and drive of the Romanian Armies. The Romanians quickly figured this out and used their air force to do reconnaissance to find these points and would concentrate their attacks on them with excellent results. The Romanian Army, coupled with the efforts of the air force and the people of the villages surrounding the battle, used the rough terrain to their advantage and carried out short and swift attacks on some of those weaker positions. Before they would make any moves though, the Romanian Army would volley a major artillery attack on the German and Austrian troops before beginning their ground and air assaults.

In August, the Romanian Army would lose support from the Russians, as the hostilities back in Russia continued to escalate and the revolution required them to return home. After a decisive counter-attack led by August von Mackensen, the Romanians and the Austrians would continue to battle back and forth, neither gaining any significant ground. This back and forth would continue until both side's reinforcements were depleted, and they had to give up and consider the Romanian Campaign a stalemate.

Eventually, over the next few weeks, Romanian cities and states would continue to fall as well as the lands that surround the nation. Eventually, this would lead to the signing of the Treaty of Brest-Litovsk, where the proud Romanian leaders and military would end up surrounded by Central Powers. In turn, this would lead to the Treaty of Bucharest in 1918, where they ceded lands to Bulgaria and bartered for peace with the German forces.

Battle of Megiddo (September 1918)

In August of 1915, the Ottoman Empire quietly joined the Central Powers and the war. In alliance with the Austro-Hungarian Empire and the newly formed German state, they hoped to be able to carve a little land out for themselves in both the Caucuses and the Balkan states. The Ottomans also wanted to regain power over the areas that once were part of the empire. Countries like Egypt and the Balkan states were among these lands. By the time the armistice was signed on October 25, both sides had lost vast numbers of soldiers, but the battle would still go down as one of the most decisive victories fought in Ottoman territory.

The first significant attack of the Ottoman campaign would be in January of 1915 on the Suez Canal. With a victory in the Sinai Peninsula, the forces, then led by General Murray, felt emboldened and pressed further into Ottoman territory in the hopes of taking Palestine. Once the British troops pushed through the Suez and into Sinai, the next two battles for Gaza came up short. These losses would be bad news for the commander of these battles because, with these losses, the powers back home decided they needed a new person leading the campaign. General Sir Edmund Allenby was the man they chose. This change of command would be significant and directly lead to the Battle of Megiddo.

Allenby brought with him a great deal of wartime experience as he had fought in the Boer War as well as the Battle of Ypres and many more. In particular, the general was well-versed with cavalry maneuvers and leading them to success. This experience gave him an advantage when it came to mobilized campaigns. He also didn't play by the rule book when it came to strategies, and that may have been the reason that the campaign was so swift and decisive. The plan he laid out to his superiors was one of these out of the box ideas. He looked to surround Gaza and gain control over Beersheba by taking the long way around. Allenby planned to drive deep into the desert and encircle Gaza. This maneuver would be the best way to spring a surprise attack on the Ottoman forces.

Though this maneuver seemed like one that was doomed to fail by many of his peers, it was just the thing that the British needed to break through and open up the possibility of taking Jerusalem. By the time the summer rolled around and the hard rode trail had been completed, it was easy for the Australian Light Horse brigades to ride in and take Beersheba. This victory opened the Gaza Strip up and left the road to Jerusalem free for the taking. Maneuvers like this had put the Ottomans on the defense. The British forces had managed to push the Ottoman forces out of Palestine, and this left them attempting to regroup and course-correct at Megiddo.

The Ottoman Army, now regrouping on the plains of Megiddo, may have thought that they were safe, but Allenby had already devised a strategic plan of attack that would take them by surprise. He wanted to trap the Ottomans on the plains and not give them any way to escape, and that was precisely what he and his troops did. The attack would be a simultaneous and coordinated attack using everything, from infantry to the cavalry, to tanks as well as planes.

The battle would start at Sharon. A group of Arab rebels, who were part of his troops, would focus on breaking the Ottoman lines of communication. At the same time, divisions of Indian and British soldiers would overrun the Ottoman forces. The battle would start with a very precise artillery bombardment, and once that was done, the infantry would push in and breach the Ottoman's defenses. After that, the Desert Mounted Cavalry (DMC) would be the third wave of attack. The Battle of Sharon was quick, and by the time night had begun to fall, many of the Ottoman strongholds and cities had fallen. That left the way open for the next essential part of Allenby's plan: an attack in the Judean Hills.

The Battle of Nablus would start with the infantry breaking through the Ottoman defenses in the hills. Along with the Chaytor's Force, a division of Allenby's troops that were comprised of both cavalry and infantry, the forces would work to take the Jordan River. At the same time, the artillery helped reduce the Ottoman Eighth Army's defenses. While all this was going on, the Ottoman Fourth would be attacked as well. The multiple pronged attacks would have battles lasting through the night. At the same time, the DMC completed their task of encircling the Ottoman troops, and this left the Ottomans open for the next phase of Allenby's plans.

Once the Ottomans had nowhere to go, all that was left was to cut off supply chains, and that meant using that new military weapon, the plane. British forces, along with their Australian compatriots, bombarded the Wadi el Fara road, the main supply chain of the Ottomans, until the Ottoman troops and divisions were defenseless.

These maneuvers allowed for the remaining British forces to easily take the Ottoman soldiers as prisoners and conquer any fortifications that were left.

Chapter Three

The Western Front

Though the fuse was lit with the archduke and his wife's assassination in mid-July of 1914, the war on the western front would not officially begin until August 3 (a week after the war started on the eastern front). The Russians' support for the Serbians had forced their hands on the eastern front, and militarization had begun. With its alliance to Austria, Germany soon declared war on Russia, but knew by doing this, they would be drawn into conflict with Russian's allies, the French. This act would give the Prussian military and the new German state the chance to enact a strategy that they had been holding in their back pocket, the Schlieffen Plan. Crafted by Alfred von Schlieffen (the former chief of staff of the German Army), this plan laid out a distinctive course of action for a two-front war that the Germans would bank on for their total victory.

On August 3, the plan came to fruition as German troops moved to the border of their neighbor and neutral nation, Belgium. Before this militarization, the German leadership had sent King Albert, the sovereign ruler of Belgium, a strongly worded suggestion that he let them pass through his territory on their march toward France. This brash tactic got the attention of the British, as Belgium had been deemed neutral. This neutrality had been in place since the signing of the Treaty of London in 1839. In response to Germany's ultimatum to the Belgian ruler, the British also sent a warning to the German governing body in Berlin to stop their plans of invasion or feel the wrath of the British military. London gave them a full day to reply, and when they had heard nothing by the deadline, the British declared war.

Neither of the sides thought the war would take long. The Kaiser even told his troops in his send-off speech that they would be home by the first week of August. There were some generals on both sides that knew different, but even with that knowledge, they did not strategically prepare for a long war. Not preparing the people or troops for this inevitability would be the biggest mistake known to man, as the war would rage on for four long years and cost millions of lives.

Battle of Marne (September 1914)

The German forces advanced across Belgium and into northeastern France, looking to capture Paris. That hope shattered with the German force's decisive and bloody defeat at the First Battle of Marne. In September of 1914, the German troops seemed to have a clear path to Paris and felt as if their conquering of this critical city was a forgone conclusion. But that celebration wouldn't be in the cards. The mass marching and insurgent attacks by divisions of the French Army would help put a tactical victory on the scoreboard for the French and their newly arrived allies, the British Expeditionary Forces (BEF).

After a month of marching through Belgium, the German Army finally crossed the Marne River and entered French territory early in September of 1914. This brazen strategy ignited fear within the French people and the government. So, to protect their assets, the French leadership made a bold move. They knew that if they stayed in Paris, the Germans would capture and torture them endlessly. The French did the only thing they could and moved their leadership south to the city of Bordeaux. Even with news of this tactical withdrawal, the Germans still felt Paris was the objective. It was the heart and cultural center of the country, and by capturing it, the Germans knew they would break the French's fighting spirit. Once that was done, the Germans would then be free to turn this attention to a much greater enemy, Russia.

The conflict waged on, victories ebbing and flowing between the two mighty empires. This initial battle of WWI could have gone either way, but thanks to some tactical miscalculations and a little luck on the French leadership part, the fight would go down as a win for the Allied Forces. The tactical miscalculation would be carried out by the leader of the First German Army, General Alexander von Kluck. But even before he could make that critical error, the French had stumbled upon a fortuitous piece of intelligence.

As the French and British forces were pulling back to regroup from one of the many small conflicts, an Allied soldier came on a fallen German infantryman. Like with any other battlefield, the Allied soldier bent down to check if the other man was still alive. Once the soldier realized that this German was dead, he began to look for supplies that he could use and found a backpack. His hands fumbled to get the bag open, but when he did, he began to rifle through it. Pulling a piece of paper out, he saw that scribbled in German across it was the battle plan that the soldier and his entire regiment were ordered to carry out.

The soldier folded the paper up and quickly found his commander to pass on the intel that he had so haphazardly found. The commander looked at the plan and realized that the French had been planning for the wrong attack. Until that moment, the French military leaders were sure that the German's First Army would march through the Oise Valley. Instead, the plan laid out in front of them showed that the Germans planned a more direct approach. The First Army would march and attack Paris head on! The leader of the French Army, Joseph Joffre, moved quickly and began to reinforce and move troops to defend their capital from the impending attack.

Using air reconnaissance and radio intercepts, which had never been done before, the French Sixth Army, led by Michel-Joseph Maunoury, moved into place, and waited. General von Kluck, getting word of the French troop movements, hurried his troops to the north to meet the advancing French forces instead of sticking with the original plan of marching on Paris straight on. This tactical choice would open the German front line up to some sound countermoves by the alliance of France and Britain. Making this decision would lead to three bloody and challenging days where the tide would continually turn along a hundred-mile stretch of land.

On September 6, General Michel-Joseph Maunoury and his Sixth Army Division, who had been standing their ground much to the chagrin of the German military leadership, received reinforcements. The close proximity to Paris had allowed for the use of public transport and taxis to help with the war effort. Over 5,000 troops arrived fresh and ready to protect their beloved Paris. Along with the soldiers, enough supplies to keep the French and British forces stocked for a little while longer also arrived. These transportation methods would become the first use of motorized transport and gained the moniker "Taxis of Marne." The preparedness of the French Army caught von Kluck by surprise, and in a matter of hours, he had moved his advanced guard back to the main body of the army. The now recombined forces raced to cut off Maunoury's troops. Unfortunately, this would lead to the German general losing contact with the Second Army lead by General Karl von Bulow, stationed on his left flank, and created a substantial breach between the two forces.

The breach created by this division of the German forces filled in with the troops of both the French Fifth Army and the BEF splitting the German forces in half. The inability of the two forces to communicate left the two German generals at a severe disadvantage when it came to outmaneuvering the Allied Forces. As the French Army began to pivot into the German's right-wing, many of the German divisions attempted with all their might to close the breach and stop Joffre's attacks. The efforts of the soldiers though were in vain, and General Bulow, just three days later, would order a retreat, understanding that this battle was lost and that there were more secure locations that his men could attack from and defend. Two days later, General von Kluck would come to the same conclusion and pull his troops back as well.

The two armies would pull back to the lower Aisne just 40 miles east from the present battlefield. The French would pursue them to the Aisne, and unfortunately, here they would lose leverage and end up in a stalemate. To prevent the Germans from losing any more ground, the German leaders would instruct their men to begin digging ditches, and so the trench warfare was born. Trying to outmaneuver and outflank each other, both forces would continue this practice and create a defensive standoff. This constant trench building would become known as the "Race to the Sea" and would leave the

French and Belgian countryside with miles and miles of barb-wired topped trenches for the next four years.

The German Army overextended both their logistical information and their firepower. Though led by a brilliant tactician, Helmuth von Moltke, the battlefield decision of his leaders left the German Army unable to reach their goal of taking control of France by invading its capital, Paris. The installation of miles and miles of trenches by the German Army was a direct response to the Schlieffen Plan's defeat and would also serve as a signal to the Allied troops that this conflict was not going to end quickly. These trenches would see some of the most inhumane circumstances and leave a whole generation scarred from diseases and psychological trauma.

Battle of Jutland (May-June 1916)

The Great War would be fought mostly on land, but the seas were not barren of epic conflicts and decisive victories. In the Spring of 1916, one of the largest and most famous battles was fought on the waters of the North Sea. The Battle of Jutland was to become the most massive naval confrontation in all of history and would hold this title until the next Great War and the Pacific Theater. The conflict would be a battle that was a tactical win for the Allies, but at such a high cost, it would be hard-pressed to call it a total victory. With 151 ships, the British Grand Fleet would square up with the German's much smaller fleet of 91 boats. The strategic goal of this maneuver was to continue blocking Germany's access to the open waters of the Atlantic. In that respect, the Battle of Jutland was an unmitigated success.

The Battle of Jutland's story starts at the very beginning of the war in 1914, in the halls of the British special intelligence agency known as Room 40. As the war began, the codes used to relay military maneuvers and troop movements were still very simple. Most relied on old-world cavalry and sailor signals that were easy to decipher and known to just about anyone. For the German military complex, the use of wireless telegraphs to send messages was new. This fact led to them not giving much attention to the code publications provided to their soldiers.

There were three publications, and luckily for the Allied troops, a copy of all three of the German codebooks was obtained very early in the war. In fact, most of the German codes were cracked before the first battles of the war even began. So, from the beginning, the British forces, both land and sea, were able to listen to every instruction relayed to the enemy troops and make tactical decisions based on them. The cracking of these codes would allow the British fleet to intercept the plans of the German Navy and help them plan accordingly.

Then in 1916, Reinhard Scheer replaced Hugo von Pohl as the chief of the High Seas Fleet, of what is now the world's second-largest naval fleet only being surpassed by their enemies, the British Grand Fleet. This change in leadership brought with it a shift in strategy (one that would eventually serve to bring the Americans into the war in 1917). Vice Admiral Scheer knew that though the German fleet was mighty, it had nothing on the British Navy's experience and size. For this reason, he moved to a lure, trap, and destroy strategy. Using this strategy would allow the German fleet to gradually dwindle the might and forces of the Royal Fleet, making the German's strategic standing better for a massive scale attack at a later date.

This strategic command translated to the directive to attack British merchant vessels. Specifically, those merchant ships that had routes that took them along the coast of Norway. It also meant planning for a logistical move to take out one of the British fleet's battlecruiser squadrons commanded by Admiral David Beatty. After deploying U-boats to key vantage points, the German High Seas Fleet set out to the north to set up on the coast of Norway. This squadron sailed with several battlecruisers as well as light cruisers commanded by Vice Admiral Franz von Hipper. At a reasonable distance behind Hipper's ships, Scheer would, with the remainder of the fleet, follow and pin Beatty between the two forces. Unfortunately, thanks to the cracking of the German naval code by the codebreakers of Room 40, Admiral John Jellicoe, the commander of the British fleet, was fully aware of the German admiral's plans and began his own countermeasures. Jellicoe intended to catch his adversary off guard and to execute a much larger scale naval maneuver.

The sun was high in the sky when the light cruisers under von Hipper's command spotted the ships of Beatty's squadron. Ready to take his adversary on, Admiral Hipper turned to face them. At 3:22 in the afternoon on May 31, the first salvos of the Battle of Jutland sailed through the air. Though ahead of schedule, this encounter seemed fortuitous to Hipper, and he looked to win his glory by drawing Beatty's ships closer to the main body of the approaching German fleet. In the first hour of the conflict, the Germans seemed to have the upper hand as they were able to sink the British vessel, the *Indefatigable*, and damage several other ships.

In response to that, Beatty moved his battlecruisers to the front. The heavy guns of the British battlecruisers lambasted the German ships, and soon Hipper's squadron was in trouble; it seemed the tides had turned. Moving to block the barrages of artillery, Hipper commanded his destroyers forward to shield the rest of the ships. As the German destroyers formed their line, they also released a flurry of torpedoes, and, in doing so, were able to sink another British battlecruiser. During the initial conflict, both sides took a considerable amount of loss and damage.

As the battle waged on, a message came through to Beatty. A British patrol squadron had spotted a large mass of German vessels heading in his direction. The plan was clear now: the German Navy was trying to sandwich Beatty between the two forces in the hopes of devastating it and weakening the position of the entire fleet. Knowing he had to react quickly, Beatty turned his ships and headed northward, where he knew Admiral Jellicoe waited. Beatty knew that not only would this help reinforce his already damaged forces but also draw the split German fleet toward a more extensive, more dominant one.

Beatty arrived at the location of Jellicoe's squadron, and both forces sat peering to the south, waiting for the Germans to be visible. Finally, 45 minutes later, at 6:15 in the evening, with the sun beginning to set, the location of the German fleet was spotted. The admiral, wanting to end this battle, swiftly radioed for his ships to form a battle line. He did not want to fight in the low light of dusk, which would heighten the danger of the conflict. With his ships anchored end to end, Jellicoe knew that the German ships would only be able to use their forward guns effectively. This strategy was a maneuver known as "Crossing the T." This fact would give the British a significant advantage when it came to firepower. As the Germans approached closer, Jellicoe and his fleet unleashed a barrage of fire, forcing Scheer to turn his vessels 180 degrees in an attempt to gain some distance between the two navies. Using a smoke screen laid out by his destroyers, Scheer scurried away in retreat. This smokescreen, coupled with the last rays of the sun, made visibility bad, and Jellicoe was left wondering what had happened.

However, the maneuvering of the British fleet had, in essence, used the very same tactic that Scheer had planned to use, and the German fleet ran smack into the rest of the British fleet just an hour later. Scheer, attempting to make the same tactical retreat as before, wound up, leaving his fleet in a worse position. Within 30 minutes of the renewed conflict, the Germans were feeling the effects of being outmaneuvered. To save the bulk of his fleet, Scheer made a Hail Mary order and deployed his torpedo boats to run headlong into the British Navy. Though this would mean losing some ships, it was a gamble that paid off as Scheer was able to turn his fleet and begin his long voyage back to his home port. Even with this tactical retreat, the two fleets would continue to have small clashes throughout the night. As the sun rose on June 1, Scheer and what remained of his fleet had been able to limp back to Wilhelmshaven, and the mighty naval battle had come to an end.

Both sides claimed victory, and in truth, both sides were victorious in their own right. The Germans sustained fewer injuries and loss of vessels. On the other hand, the British had lost somewhere in the realm of 6,100 men and several ships that would equate out to about 113 tons of metal. The Germans had only lost about 2,500 men and 62,300 tons. When it comes to achieving their ultimate goal, however, the British were the winners. They were able to maintain their blockade on the Germans, and that meant keeping the German fleet from having access to the open seas and more merchant routes.

Battle of Verdun (February-December 1916)

The Battle of Verdun would end up being one of the most bloody and lengthy offensives in the war. It would see troops moving into enemy trenches as the lines moved forward and backward, having to live in squalid surroundings with heaps of decomposing bodies. The battlefield would end up with dead soldiers beaten to bloody messes from heavy barrages of artillery strewn across miles of the French countryside. These fields would be home to some of the most horrific atrocities of the war. This campaign would be a war of attrition. By the time the 11-month battle was over, there would be over 700,000 casualties. This carnage was the result of the mindset and tactics of a prominent German military mind, General Erich von Falkenhayn.

General Erich von Falkenhayn would send word to the Kaiser himself and lay out how he thought the Germans could win the western front. The general argued that Britain was definitely formidable but that taking Britain would only be possible with the use of U-boats, and that would be difficult with the British strength when it came to their navy. Instead, mercilessly attacking the French and inflicting so much torment and damage on their ally, France, would be the only way to get Britain to the peace table and win the war on that front. So, taking France was the key to either a German victory or defeat. There would be no stealthy maneuvers and could be no peace treaties. Instead, the only way this war would be won, Falkenhayn believed, was to inflict as much damage as possible, both when it came to property and human lives.

Thus, attrition would be the name of the game if Germany hoped to take France. This notion was not a well-received one. However, the Kaiser eventually approved the campaign, despite his and the other leaders' misgivings. The defeat of this crucial part of the Allied Forces would not come with mass troop movements into their territory, rather a strategic choice of location and then the constant barrage of attacks that would bleed France into submission. They would need to choose the right site for the battle first. The chosen site had to be a place that could break not only the French Army's spirit but also its power as well. The best option would be a symbolic location that the French would give their lives to protect and one that would benefit the future movements of German soldiers into the French countryside. After studying the maps, Falkenhayn settled on Verdun.

Not only was Verdun a tactical gem, but it was also a precious sight for the French people and a significant location for the Germans as well. For the Germans, the town held a special place in their hearts as it was the site of the signing of the Treaty of Verdun in 843 A.D. The signing of this treaty would split the Carolingian Empire up. This separation would help create the states that later became the core of what was the new German nation. The ancient city was also one of the last occupied by the Germans in the Franco-Prussian War. After the loss and formation of a new German border, the French built the city into a heavily fortified stronghold to protect it from future German aggression. The Verdun fortress along the Meuse was threatening German communications as well, which needed to be taken care of immediately. By occupying this citadel, the German forces would be killing two birds with the same stone—taking a strategic point on the front line and dealing a death blow to the French. Or at least that is what Falkenhayn thought.

To maximize the efficiency of the general's plan and the landscape, the Germans would have to attack with several rapid burst advancements. This tactic would serve to pull the French reserves to the front and directly into the extensive artillery line put in place by the Germans. To start these advancements, rapid and intense artillery barrages would be executed. This tactic would allow the Germans troops to move quickly and shore up the land gain before the French could bring more reserves to the front or plan a counter-attack. Once the plan was finalized, it was then laid out for the operations commander, Prince Wilhelm, the oldest son of the Prussian ruler. The Prince had little military experience and was swayed by the passion and conviction of Falkenhayn. The first stage would be to shore up their forces in the vicinity of Verdun, and doing so without being seen would be difficult.

Over several weeks, Falkenhayn and the commanders of the army began moving artillery and troops forward using the hilly landscape and air cover to keep their movements secret. But first, they would need transportation and shelter, and this was done by building a railway line as well as concrete bunkers at the destination site. With these in place, Falkenhayn and Prince Wilhelm began moving their supplies and armaments. The Germans, over several weeks, were able to move several tons of artillery and munitions, not to mention thousands of troops and all under the not so watchful eyes of the French forces stationed in the region.

It wasn't until early January that French reconnaissance planes noticed that there had been some ramping up of German troops, but at the time, the French didn't seem to be too concerned. Then in early February, the news of the size of the German build-up on the banks of Meuse was relayed properly to French intelligence. With this new intel conveyed to the leaders of the French Army, they began to improve the defensive capability of the Verdun region hastily. To slow this process down, the German forces started to cut off access to the central railways. The French quickly course-corrected. Instead of using the railways, they began to use the "Marne Taxi" idea and developed routes for a motorized supply chain. This 37-mile road (which would become known as the La Voie Sacrée) would be a crucial part of the French defenses for the entirety of this brutal conflict. It took over a week for the French to get supplies to their front line because of the German machinations. But in that time, large quantities of weapons and men were moved to the front, and the French felt they were ready for whatever the Germans would bring, but they were wrong.

With both armies in place, in the early hours of February 21, the Germans began to execute their plan. With 25 miles of front line armed with massive artillery, they began to bombard the French. When the initial hail of artillery finished, the Germans sent out scouts to investigate the damage. If the French defense were devastated, German scouts would signal for a push of the infantry, and if the defenses hadn't been crushed, the message would be sent to begin the artillery bombardment once again. In the late afternoon, the defense was finally ripe for the picking, and the German infantry began to push forward, followed by combat engineers and then the main body of the German forces. This process would repeat multiple times until the field was covered with piles of corpses and the enemy driven back. Over the next few days, the German military gained quite a bit of leverage breaking through the first line of the French defenses. The troops and supplies had been depleted. Both sides took some time and rushed to bolster their positions as well as forces.

Though the French during the initial German push were able to save one city, the rest of the French defenses were wiped out rather quickly. The significant loss to the Germans caused the higher-ups in the French government and military to reconsider the leadership at the front. They would replace the "Victor of Marne," General Joffre, with General Pétain. This change of command also came with a fresh and ready-to-fight army. The task for these new troops was to hold the right bank no matter what. Though initially, the powers-at-be wanted to amass the French forces on the left bank to stop the Germans from crossing, the higher ground of the right bank was thought to be easier to defend.

Four days after the first battle, the Germans neared Fort Douaumont, which was one of the fortifications built up after the Franco-Prussian War. The French, busy with their troop movements, never saw the attack coming. The Germans quietly approached the bastion and found a passageway that was left unguarded. The small squadron worked their way into the catacombs under the city and was able to, without spilling any blood, round up the 57 French soldiers left to man the fortress. This victory was bloodless and would be celebrated by Germans near and far. The Germans would hold this fort for eight months before the French were able to regain the stronghold. Eventually, the retaking of Fort Douaumont would be one of the victories that would turn the tides of the battle. Taking this tactical position back was followed by the French chasing the German Air Force out of the skies over Verdun. The Germans would mount a counter-attack, but even after that, the French held firm at Douaumont.

In June, the Germans would receive the news that the eastern front had taken a huge hit. Russian General Brusilov (see Chapter 2: The Eastern Front - Brusilov Offensive) had just unleashed a devastating defeat to the Austro-Hungarian forces. Moving these troops would mean that many of the resources destined for the Battle of Verdun were diverted to the front line in Ukraine. The final French Summer Offensive was unleashed on June 24 and commenced with an artillery bombardment that lasted a full week. Then the infantry pushed in after this. The Germans were able to repel it but took heavy casualties (as did the Allies). The back and forth advance and retreat continued for the next few months, but in September, the tides would turn in favor of the French and their allies. Then came the news that the British were converging on Somme, and with this two-pronged attack spurred on by the pleading of the French generals, the death knell had begun to ring for the Battle of Verdun (though it would take another four months to end ultimately).

Eventually, in mid-September, one of the French generals that had helped maintain the line of the right bank proposed a strategy that would deliver Verdun back into the hands of the Allies. General Charles Mangin suggested using similar tactics as his German counterparts had used to gain their foothold. The movement would start with a massive artillery bombardment followed by an infantry insurgence. With the reduced forces due to both the Battle of Somme and the Brusilov Offensive, it wasn't long before the French had taken back several of the cities that had fallen into German hands over the last several months.

The general, who was okay with the loss of his men, would attempt the same tactic in early December. However, the weather would postpone that maneuver. This little hiccup allowed the Germans to learn of the plan and launch their own counter-attack. This preemption wouldn't last long, and soon both sides were under furious fire from their enemies. On December 18, the French would reclaim Chambrettes and capture thousands of German soldiers to end the battle that had raged on for almost a year.

German Spring Offensive (March-July 1918)

As the war began to wear down, the troops on both sides felt the fatigue and psychological effects of fighting for almost four straight years. Knowing this, the leaders of the German military attempted one last push. The goal of the Spring Offensive was to deliver a definitive blow to the allies and reinvigorate the German military force. The plan for the offensive began in late 1917, when General Erich von Ludendorff, the First Quartermaster General, began to consider a reinvigorated offensive strategy.

With the looming inclusion of America's massive army and the collapse of the war efforts on the eastern front due to the victorious Russian Revolution, Germany was able to reallocate resources. Because of these factors, it made sense to plan an offensive. There would only be one shot, though, as the attack is needed to be executed before the U.S. could replenish their troops. With the decision finalized and approved by Ludendorff's commanders, the general began to plan this offensive.

The German tactician selected a 50-mile stretch of the front line that was defended by the British Army. Attacking the British Army instead of the French was a calculated tactic and one that, if the general had set a territorial objective, may have just worked. The British military was less war-experienced than the French or the Germans, and this led the Germans to look at them as easy pickings.

The miscalculation of not defining territorial objectives allowed the general to miss out on some strategic points that could have turned the tides of not only this conflict but also the war in general. Vital weak points like the vulnerability of the British at the rail hubs of Hazebrouck and Amiens could have been substantial targets if he had focused his troop's efforts on them. This concentration on the weak points would have allowed Ludendorff the ability to cut the British off from supplies and reinforcements.

Instead of focusing on these strategic points, Ludendorff went into the mission with two distinct goals. The general wanted to push his way in between the French and British Armies. Once this had been accomplished, with the less-experienced British Army separated from the French, the general planned to move north and annihilate the British line. Lastly, he planned to use psychological warfare and tactical advantages to Germany's benefit. Once separated from the French, who were familiar with more combat tactics than trench warfare, Ludendorff felt the British would be easy to defeat and quick to surrender.

Once Operation Michael's plan (the Germans' codename for the first phase of the Spring Offensive) was finalized, all that was left was to choose the time. On March 21, 1918, in the early morning hours, the Germans moved onto that 50-mile stretch of the Allies' line chosen by Ludendorff as the objective. The British forces had been alerted to the attack but were unprepared for the newly-reinforced German military and the might of their artillery. With heavy barrages of artillery and blazes of bullets, the Germans launched their attack, aided by the dense fog that blanketed the land that morning. For five hours, this constant bombardment went on, and once the general felt that the line was significantly weakened, the infantry and cavalry moved through the line.

The initial result was excellent, with the German military advancing over quite a distance thanks to their month-long training to prepare for the offensive. When the initial push of the assault was complete, the Germans had taken a good amount of land and almost 100,000 prisoners. This "victory" was not one at all though, as Ludendorff had made one significant error. After this advancement, he assumed the British Army had been defeated and moved several units to the south to stop the French from sending reinforcements. This decision split his force and left his attacks less impactful, which would hurt the campaign significantly in the long run. Though the first phase of the offensive technically was a success due to the land gained, none of the lands that had been acquired held any tactical or strategic value.

After the initial push, the Germans would repeat this tactic down the 50-mile stretch of the front line. Each of the subsequent offensives (codenames Operation Georgette and Blücher) were failures for Ludendorff and his troops. Whether it was from tactical errors, like splitting his army up, or being tricked into launching a full attack when he didn't have the resources, the rest of the Spring Offensive would see defeat after defeat for Ludendorff and the German Army. On July 18, the French moved on the weakened German forces in a surprise attack, and from then on, the war was in complete control of the Allies, and the Spring Offensive had been crushed.

Battle of Amiens (August 1918)

The Battle of Amiens would be one of the final battles of the war and was the first of the Allied offensive that would come to be called the "Hundred Days" campaign. The Battle of Amiens was a direct result of the ineffectiveness of the German Spring Offensive. With the failure of Ludendorff's Spring Offensive, the Allied Forces looked to execute their own campaign. The inability to capture Amiens as a critical tactical point due to the railway hub by Ludendorff left General von der Marwitz in a little bit of bind. That, coupled with the unsuccessful last German offensive at the Second Battle of Marne, left the German Army open for an Allied push. The Allied invasion would aim at securing and retaking strategic hubs such as Amiens, which would allow them to move supplies and troops more effectively. The Allied Forces would be reinforced with troops from several nations, including the U.S.

General Ferdinand Foch understood the need for an offensive with this objective and looked for the first acquisition to be the securing of the railway hub at Amiens, which was a vital line to Paris. In August, along with his allies, Foch began consistent and rapid attacks on the German line. These attacks would leave the Germans little to no time to recover and would be the deciding factor in the war. While these attacks went on, troops had deployed to bolster the forces of the Fourth Army commanded by General Sir Henry Rawlinson that would move on Marwitz when ready.

When it was all said and done, one of his units included 14 infantry divisions made up of soldiers of Australia, Britain, Canada, and the U.S. He also had control over tank units and cavalry as well. These nightly exercises would give him the element of surprise and be one of the things that gave the Allied Forces such an advantage over their German adversaries at the Battle of Amiens.

Armed with many tanks and guns, the forces were supported with aircraft from both the British and French. This massive army was to face Marwitz's Second Army, which was comprised of ten divisions with limited supplies and equipment. Coupled with the demoralization of the German Army after the Spring Offensive, the stage was set for an Allied victory. On August 8, in the early morning hours under cover of fog, the British began their attack. Over the next few hours, the advancement of the Allied troops would show their might and destroy the first German defensive line. In a later memoir, Ludendorff would call August 8 as the "Black Day." This battle gave the Allies territory, but the demoralization of the German troops is what Ludendorff refers to with this moniker.

Other parts of the offensive did not fare as well, but on the whole, the Battle of Amiens was a success. By August 12, the Allies seemed to have gained all they could, and Field Marshall Haig called the battle done and moved to prepare an offensive to the north. The fighting would continue for several more months, but shortly after this Allied victory, many German higher-ups, including the Kaiser himself, had already accepted their defeat.

Chapter Four

Heroes of WWI

When it comes to defining what makes a hero, it can be tough. Is it the soldier who follows his orders even when he doesn't agree with them? Or the soldier who goes against the rules to ensure his men get home safe? Is it the nurse that risks her life to save innocents from the terrors of war? Or is it the pilot who heroically takes down multiple enemies, protecting his people and furthering his country's cause?

The truth is, these situations can all be called heroism, and WWI has some fantastic stories when it comes to bravery and those who put their life in the line of danger for others and their country. These stories below are of people that come from many different backgrounds and fought on both sides. Still, one thing is for sure, for whatever side they fought on, they were heroes that showed courage and conviction in the face of unknown terror.

Baron Manfred von Richthofen – The "Red Baron"

Known to the world as the "Red Baron," Manfred von Richthofen was born into a well-respected Prussian military family. He would also become one of the biggest heroes of the German people during WWI. Living by the motto "Go for the lead pilot first" between 1916 and 1918, the flying ace would gain notoriety by shooting down 80 Allied aircraft. The Allied pilots that flew through the skies over the battlefields feared looking out at the horizon and seeing the Baron's patented red plane, knowing that this may very well be the end for them. His precision and ruthlessness would end up making him a propaganda machine for the Germans and turn him into a national hero.

Born into a noble Prussian family in the Spring of 1892, it was a foregone conclusion that he would find himself standing in the Prussian military complex. Spending his youth hunting and playing sports, young Baron Richthofen would appease his stern and proud Prussian father by enrolling in military school at the very young age of 11. Here, he would continue to excel, and by the time he was 17, he would have his first commission.

Working his way through the grades, he would graduate in 1911 and was assigned to a cavalry regiment. When the war broke out, his unit saw action on both the front line of the western and eastern fronts. It was there that he began to make a name for himself. With bravery and dedication, he and his cavalry unit would travel along the front lines, and for his courage, he earned an Iron Cross.

The war quickly turned, and eventually, his cavalry unit was assigned the mission of maintaining and distributing supplies up and down the trenches of the western front. The repetitive, tedious assignment felt to Richthofen a little too menial for a Prussian of his standing. So, he appealed to the higher-ups to transfer him to the German Air Service. The German command, because of his reputation, approved this, and Richthofen would find himself as a backseat observer in the reconnaissance planes of the German Air Service.

Sent to do reconnaissance on the eastern front, Richthofen would take the summer of 1915 to earn his pilot license in between his reconnaissance missions. The transition between the backseat and the front seat was challenging (he even crashed on his first solo flight), but Richthofen pushed through the process. Once he had his license, he began taking combat missions over France and Russia. During these missions, he met the famed pilot, Oswald Boelcke, who saw potential and recruited him into the newly formed fighter squadron, Jasta 2.

It wasn't long until he had absorbed everything that he could from the seasoned fighter pilot and began building the reputation he would become known for, including gaining the title of flying ace after his first confirmed aerial victory in September of 1916. Richthofen would rack up quite a tally over the coming month, having 16 confirmed victories, putting him squarely on the top of the leaderboard. The German ace was so proud of his work that he felt he needed to commemorate his triumphs. So Richthofen sent word back to a Berlin craftsman and started having silver cups created for each of his aerial victories. He would amass 60 of these before the silver shortage would put an end to this practice.

Because of his fearless work on behalf of the German military, he earned the highest honor a military man could receive, the "Blue Max," and command of his fighting squadron, the Jasta 11. It was at this time he decided he needed to make a change and painted his plane that iconic red that the pilot would be known for, and that would birth the moniker he would go down in history with, the "Red Baron."

The "Red Baron" would have a stellar season in the spring if 1917. He would take down another 36 enemy planes to bring his total up to 52. It was clear he was approaching legendary status, and the German leadership began to realize he was the perfect propaganda tool. Hence, they started handing him every military decoration they could and put his face on newspapers, magazines, and even postcards. Soon the "Red Baron," a symbol of German excellence and pride, was whom every little German boy wanted to be, and every German girl wanted to marry.

After a productive spring for him and his squadron, Richthofen got another promotion and took charge of his very own fighter wing, Jagdgeschwader 1, otherwise known as the "Flying Circus." Taking a cue from their leader, the squadron decided to paint their aircraft with bright colors, and the pilots chosen for this division were, like the Baron, able to fly effortlessly through the air, much like a trapeze artist did through the air of the big top. It would be at this time that the Baron began flying the red triplane that would be his most famous aircraft.

The legend would come to an end in April of 1918. Engaging a squadron of British planes flying over the Somme Valley in France, he and his squad would battle bravely through the air. As Richthofen swooped down low to follow his target, Australian machine gunfire sprayed from the ground, surprising the pilot. The ground fire, combined with the fire from the Canadian pilot Arthur Roy Brown, would have the German flying ace on the run. During the barrage of gunfire, Richthofen would take a bullet straight to his upper body and plunge headfirst to the field below.

Crashed behind enemy lines, the German flying ace's body was recovered by the Allies and given a respectful and proper burial that would suit his heroic status. The legend was dead, and for the Allied pilots, the skies would be a little safer.

Edith Cavell

The hero nurse of Belgium, Edith Cavell, fought to keep soldiers alive to the very end. Standing up for what she believed, this soft-spoken nurse would save over 200 men's lives and help them get safely out of occupied Belgium. But she did not discriminate; she fearlessly lived by the motto, "I must have no hatred or bitterness towards anyone." This dedication to saving lives came later in life but would be the attribute that wrote her name in the annals of history and tragically would bring about the end of her life.

Edith was born in 1865 and spent the first quarter of her life walking the streets of Swardeston in Norfolk, England. She worked as a nanny, but this was not fulfilling nor what she wanted to do for the rest of her life. She was a caring young lady but wanted to find a path of her own. Then tragedy would befall her father, and being the oldest child, Edith took on the duty of nursing him through his severe illness. As she diligently oversaw his recovery, she soon realized that she had finally found her calling: nursing.

Edith, now sure that medicine was her future, began to find places and classes to learn everything she needed to be a successful nurse. She worked in several hospitals throughout London and soon became well-known amongst them. A visiting surgeon from Brussels worked alongside her and saw the potential and the care Edith gave her patients. He urged her to join him back in Brussels, and with some serious convincing, she decided that it was an excellent opportunity.

In 1907, Edith moved from her native country to Belgium. It wasn't long before she had built up a reputation. The surgeon who had convinced her to uproot her life also suggested that Edith begin training nurses as her bedside manner was just what every ailing individual would need and want. So, she took his advice here as well and began to teach her skills and methods to other young women. Eventually, it led to the founding of the Berkendael Institute, Belgium's first nursing school.

In 1914 however, things were going to change drastically. Belgium was in the direct line of the German Army's plans to take France. As the German troops advanced through Belgium, they also occupied it, feeling as it would give them a strategic advantage over both the French and the British. With an occupied Belgium, they could have a clear path for reinforcements and a strategic post to watch their enemy movements closely.

Edith Cavell, a citizen of one of these adversaries, would seem like a dangerous person to leave amidst your newly conquered lands. But with the school becoming a Red Cross hospital, the Germans had no recourse (at the time) to remove her. Though they had no way of relieving Edith of her post, the Germans did not trust her (or any of the nurse and staff of the hospital), so the Germans, using spies and informants, would continually monitor movement within the institute's walls. So, Edith's school was allowed to remain open and would begin treating soldiers from both sides.

Edith Cavell could have abandoned her post, but she knew that she was needed, so she stayed. Eventually, she would join the Belgian Underground and begin rescuing Allied soldiers stuck behind enemy lines. Cavell used her institute to house these soldiers and used her ingenuity and wits to throw the Germans off their trail. Along with her compatriots, she created an underground path that led to Holland and then back to England, which allowed many men to find their way back home and to safety.

Cavell rescued hundreds of soldiers before the German spies that watched her discovered her betrayal and began to make preparations to end her extracurricular activities. In August of 1915, the Germans had accrued enough information to accuse Cavell of what they felt was a horrible betrayal of their trust. She was arrested and charged with treason. Taken to St. Gilles Prison in Brussels, she would await her trial.

Nearly a month later, her trial would finally begin. During her hearing, she was asked a handful of questions, and with confidence and dignity, answered honestly. Question after question was asked of her, and each she answered with full voice. Then, she was asked how many soldiers she spirited away to safety. She straightened her back and spoke clearly, "I have saved hundreds of lives and would not hesitate to do so again!" This question would be one of the last items asked of her. Deliberation was quick, and sentencing was even quicker. Edith Cavell had been found guilty of treason and was sentenced to death by firing squad.

On October 12, Edith Cavell and other conspirators were taken out to a courtyard, and in a hail of bullets, their lives would come to a tragic end. When word of this execution became known to the world, it caused outrage, and for her bravery, she has been remembered ever since.

Aníbal Milhais

When most people think of the combatants of WWI, they think of Germany, Austria, France, England, and even the U.S., but many other countries sent troops to the front line. One of those was Portugal, which had abstained from the war for the first two years. However, the neutral nation had no choice but to enter once Germany surprisingly declared war on them in 1916. Portugal quickly mounted a large force and sent them bravely into battle in France. It seemed that the Portuguese knew this was potentially going to happen. In

1915, the nation had begun drafting soldiers into the army to build its ranks. Among these men was a humble farmer named Aníbal Milhais. This quiet young man was drafted into the Second Division and would eventually find himself deployed to France in 1917.

By April of 1918, Milhais' unit had seen nine months of action and was ready to be rotated out. Tired and emotionally drained, Aníbal and his platoon were prepared to go home and see their loved ones, but fate had different plans. The company had been taking heavy fire for days, and the Germans had moved their troops up in preparation for one last push (see Chapter 3: The Western Front - German Spring Offensive). The stage was set for a long and bloody battle, and Aníbal's units were smack dab in the middle of it. This battle would become known as the Battle of Lys.

Unfortunately, when the Battle of Lys started, Milhais and another soldier found themselves behind enemy lines. As the two of them sat at the bottom of a hill sheltering themselves from the artillery fire of the two previous days, gunshots rang out. The two soldiers climbed the hill they had been stuck behind trying to get to higher ground to see what was happening. As they topped the crest of the hill, they were greeted with a view of their battalion in full retreat. Knowing that they needed to make it back to their unit, the two Portuguese soldiers began their treacherous journey down the hill and back to their countrymen.

Along with the gunfire, the German soldiers were lobbing grenades into the retreating Portuguese troops. As Aníbal and his compatriot weaved through the broken landscape, one of those grenades landed near their path. The explosion was loud and tragically exploded close to the other soldier, killing him. To keep that from happening to him as well, Aníbal sheltered himself, and once the grenade explosions stopped, left the safety of his shelter only to find that the German forces had almost taken the hill he now stood on.

As he took in this sight, the Portuguese soldier knew that his brothers-in-arms would need more time to retreat. Reacting quickly to this unthinkable predicament, Aníbal stood up and reached for his Lewis machine gun. Standing on that hill, looking down at the fury of the German soldiers, he lifted his weapon and began firing. He moved from place to place on the hill, continually firing, hoping that the tactic would trick the Germans into believing that there were more soldiers than just him on that hill.

Feeling that the hill wasn't worth the loss of German soldiers, the German commander instructed his men to forget taking the hill and instead kept moving on their objective. Milhais would not stop, though; he continued firing on the enemy until he had no bullets left. The soldier found himself alone, behind enemy lines, with no ammunition. He knew that if he stayed in place, he was sure to be spotted, and so for three days, he kept on the move, hoping to find his way back to his unit eventually. On the third day, he stumbled upon a Scottish officer who had found himself in the same predicament, and together they found their way back to Allied territory.

Aníbal never spoke to anyone about what he had done, and his bravery would have gone unknown if not for a report filed by that Scottish officer. Aníbal would go on to earn several medals and return to his country a hero.

Ecaterina Teodoroiu

Born in a small village called Vădeni, young Ecaterina would have never guessed where life would lead her. Her fate would be far from what she dreamed. After four years of school, she moved on to a girl's school in Bucharest, where she studied to be a teacher. But in 1916, the Kingdom of Romania joined the war, and her destiny was written in stone. Course-correcting her life, she moved from preparing to become a teacher to serving her country, and that change in the path would leave her one of the greatest Romanian heroes of the war.

Over the years, Ecaterina had worked as both a scout and a nurse, and wanting to contribute to the effort, chose to use this experience on the front lines. The devoted patriot worked along with reserves forces and civilians at the Jiu River. Banding together, the Romanian troops stationed with her were able to hold the advancing German forces back. Charged with caring for the fallen soldiers, Ecaterina soon developed a respect for the level of patriotism that even the wounded had, and this patriotism was contagious. Tragedy would strike again, and fate would urge Ecaterina to course-correct. Word that her brother had fallen on the front line reached her, and this stirred the fire inside Ecaterina. The Romanian nurse chose a bold move for a woman at this time; she requested to be a front-line soldier. With reluctance, she was granted her wish and moved to the front to serve with the 18th Infantry Regiment.

Ecaterina was a smart woman, and because of this, she adapted to the strategic thinking of military life easily and quickly. This adaptability led her to assist in planning and to make some quick decisions when faced with difficult situations. For instance, at one point, her unit, surrounded by German soldiers, was in danger of being captured. With a quick wit and a masterful plan, she was able to fool the Germans and keep her comrades from being taken as prisoners.

Unfortunately, eventually, her smarts and tricks would run out, and she too would end up captured. It wouldn't be long before she began to formulate a plan to free herself from her German captives. Unbeknownst to the Germans, Ecaterina had managed to conceal a revolver from them. She waited for the perfect moment and then sprung on the soldiers guarding her. Fighting her way free, Ecaterina managed to get several shots and ended up killing two German soldiers. Finally free, she realized she had been hit, but it was a mere flesh wound, and she worked her way back to the front lines.

Over the next few days, Ecaterina's battalion would see plenty of combat, and eventually, Ecaterina would suffer an injury bad enough to take her off the battlefield. The injured soldier would be moved to a hospital in Iasi for a month while her wound healed. Once she was released, Ecaterina hurried back to the front line under the command of a new leader, Lieutenant Mănoiu. She would return not as a soldier, though, but as a nurse stationed with his infantry regiment. Her bravery even in this non-combatant role earned her many accolades, and eventually, she was made an Honorary Second Lieutenant and given command of a 25-man platoon.

Her battalion would see a lot of action as they moved their way closer to the front line. On August 17, as the battles became harsher and neared the end of the Romanian campaign, her commander asked her to stay behind at the mobile hospital. She refused and instead continued the move with her men.

Almost a month later, the Romanian lines were attacked by the Germans. While leading a counterstrike, Lieutenant Teodoroiu was struck in the chest or head—stories conflict—and she died on the battlefield.

Some say her final words were, "Forward men, I'm still with you!" The memory of Ecaterina Teodoroiu would live on and become a symbol of true Romanian patriotism and strength.

Edouard Izac

Edouard Izac was born to German immigrant parents in 1891 in Iowa. Being born to parents that spoke very little to no

English meant that German was spoken in his home. So young Edouard was bilingual, which would be a good thing in the Spring of 1918. Izac would end up being a prisoner of war and use his knowledge of the German language to obtain information. Unfortunately for him, he was never able to use that knowledge as he would end up a prisoner for the remaining months of the war. But his heroic efforts and dedication to his country would be honored for decades to come.

Edouard Izac graduated from Annapolis in 1915 and was assigned to duty on the battleship *USS Florida*. Until the sinking of the *Lusitania* and the interception of the Zimmermann Telegram, it looked like the U.S. would be able to stay neutral through the war. However, with these two events, it was clear that the country could no longer avoid conflict. As the country geared up for a fight, the naval transport service needed new blood, and Izac was reassigned to the *USS President Lincoln*. This ship would be used to ferry American troops and equipment to the shores of Europe to aid the U.S. allies.

After several successful transports across the Atlantic, Izac was promoted to the ship's executive officer. Having just unloaded its fifth batch of troops, the ship was getting ready to turn around and return to the shores of the U.S. to pick up another load. The seas seemed calm as the boat entered open waters. But early the following morning, Lincoln's crew was shaken awake by massive vibrations that echoed through the bows of the ship. The ship had been struck from the side by three torpedoes from a hidden German U-boat. The crew rushed to the lifeboats and watched as the boat sunk rapidly. With the crew safely in the lifeboats, the leadership was unaware of the tragedy that was yet to come. Several feet away from the lifeboats, the U-boat that had sunk their ship surfaced.

The commander of the U-boat emerged, and escorted by his men demanded the *Lincoln*'s captain be turned over to prove to their commanders back home that they had sunk this ship. Izac, wanting to save his men from any further tragedy, stood up and told the German commander that their captain had gone down with the ship. With the captain dead, the Germans settled for the executive officer, and Izac was brought on board the submarine as a prisoner of war.

The Germans set Izac up with his own room and treated him with respect. But, unaware that Edouard spoke German, they also had no problem discussing sensitive material in front of him, and Izac soon realized this could be a significant advantage to the Allied war efforts. The sailor began listening intently and taking mental note of every little detail he thought could be used to aid his fellow soldiers once he escaped. Once the U-boat made its way back to their home base, Izac was moved to a POW camp.

While housed in this POW camp, Izac would not rest on his laurels. He knew he had information that was vital and needed to be delivered to the Allied commanders. So, he made several attempts to escape but failed every time. After being in that camp for a month, the German command decided that he needed to be moved to a new camp. Thinking this was a perfect moment, Izac attempted yet another escape. Midway through the transport, he made his move and was able to get away. Eventually, he was recaptured and beaten severely and taken on to the next camp. It was from this camp that he would make his final escape and find his way to Switzerland.

Unfortunately, he was unable to relay the critical information he had acquired during his time on the German submarine, as he found his way to the authorities on the very day that war ended, November 11, 1918. Though the delivery was too late, this sailor's stubbornness and desire to assist his country was truly heroic.

Chapter Five

Stories & Events

History is a series of moments and events; the stories within these moments are what bring that history to life, long after all is said and done. The stories of the Great War are many and full of epic battles, daring courage and heroic deeds that show the strength and the will of humanity.

There are so many stories to choose from and so much to be learned by studying them. After all, according to George Santayana, "Those who cannot remember the past are condemned to repeat it." These stories will allow you to remember what the people of that time were going through and how their strife and tragedy built the world we live in today.

The Sinking of the *Lusitania*

Many passenger ships would be commissioned to join the war efforts. The *Lusitania*, a British passenger ship, was one of these. It would still be used to transport passengers, but in 1914, would also be secretly modified to carry supplies and troops as well. By 1915, the German military command was well aware that British passenger ships were being used to ferry troops and arms across the Atlantic from the U.S. to the shores of the European continent to bolster the Allied efforts.

To the German naval commanders, this meant that these ships were fair game, and they had no problem making passenger and merchant ships targets of their U-boats. Knowing that America's interference would be a problem, the German embassy used the media outlets within the U.S. to help deter passengers from making the journey across the ocean. In 1915, a campaign was distributed in the U.S., warning the citizens that there was a war going on between the two European nations. That any person on one of the British passenger ships would then be an enemy of the German state, and they would be in danger of potential attacks. So, if the American public wanted to remain safe, they would avoid these ships at all costs.

These warnings fell on deaf ears as most assumed that the Germans would abide by common decency and allow any survivors to make it to lifeboats. Those assumptions turned out to be very wrong. Six days into the *Lusitania*'s voyage, in the early afternoon of May 7, off the coast of Ireland, the *Lusitania* was struck by a torpedo without any kind of warning, and quickly sank to the ocean floor.

The torpedo ripped through the bow of the passenger ship, opening up the hull, allowing tons of seawater to rush into the gaping hole rapidly. Within seconds of the initial strike, a secondary explosion rocked the ship, and this is what sealed the fate of the mighty ocean liner. In just 20 minutes, the boat was no longer visible. The ship sank so quickly that there was no time for many of the passengers or crew to escape to the lifeboats. Of the almost 2,000 people on board, approximately 760 survived. Even with this blatant disregard for human life, the Americans tried to maintain their neutrality.

There was outrage across the globe. Germany vehemently defended their actions by saying that the *Lusitania* carried weapons, which made it a war vessel, and therefore it was perfectly acceptable to take action against it. The media announcement of this outlandish claim only stirred up Britain's war propaganda machine. In the coming weeks, more

British citizens headed to the recruiting stations to sign up to fight against the ruthless Germans. Along with this surge of patriotism, there came riots in the streets of London.

However, it would take more than one passenger ship sinking to get the U.S. to break their neutrality. Not long after the tragedy of the *Lusitania*, the Germans hit another vessel, and the U.S. knew they had to react with some sort of warning, so they cut off all diplomatic ties with Germany. With these two sinkings and the interception of the Zimmermann Telegram, there was no doubt that America's decision to declare war on Germany was justified and necessary.

The Christmas Truce

The war had been raging for five months (longer than most had predicted when it began), and the holiday season was coming quickly. So, to show goodwill to all men, a suggestion was issued from the walls of the Vatican. Pope Benedict XV wanted both sides to lay down their arms so that the birth of their savior could be celebrated without bloodshed. Neither side's leadership, though, took much notice of the papal suggestion. But as the stars began to shine on Christmas Eve, there were some signs that despite their commander's lack of support, the troops on both sides felt the same way.

Whether it was in response to the Pope's edict or just the soldiers missing their families and wanting a little reminder of them will never be known. As the breeze blew across the broken and corpse-filled fields, a noise began to waft across the fields. From the trenches on both sides of No Man's Land, Christmas carols began to ring out (some even accompanied by instruments according to some stories). The singing would continue into the late hours of the evening.

When the sun began to rise on Christmas Day, as the allied troops prepared for another long day of combat and tragedy, they began to hear distant murmurs that seemed like a familiar greeting. Over the distance, many of the soldiers thought they could hear someone wishing them a Merry Christmas. As they stuck their heads slowly over the trenches, German troops could be seen coming across No Man's Land, and as the enemy got closer, the Allied soldiers could more clearly make out the words, and it was the Merry Christmas that they had been hearing.

At first, the Allied soldiers thought that this could be a trick, but when the Germans got close enough, they could see that these troops were unarmed and genuinely wanted to have a day of celebration. With this realization, the Allied Forces began to emerge from their trenches as well—the soldiers, who, just days before, had been mercilessly killing each other, celebrated together.

The soldiers would do everything that they would typically do on Christmas morning. They exchanged gifts, played friendly soccer games, sang carols, and decorated trees. Though they didn't have much, they exchanged what they had, which meant things like cigarettes and even plum puddings. The day was filled with laughter and camaraderie.

With the cease-fire, some unfortunate tasks were also completed—things like retrieval of fallen soldiers from No Man's Land and treatment of unattended injuries. After a full day of camaraderie, the two sides returned to their trenches and prepared for the battle to begin again the next morning.

Japan Declares War

Just days after the British declared war on Germany, the British foreign secretary, looking to take advantage of an alliance agreement signed years before, reached out to the Japanese leadership for help. Sir Edward Grey needed the Japanese to use their impressive navy to scout out German merchant ships that may be carrying supplies and weapons to the German forces. This request played right into the political aspiration of the Japanese as they wanted to expand their footprint in the Far East. Living up to their words in the 1902 Alliance Treaty, the Japanese acted swiftly, drawing a line in the sand with the German forces stationed at naval bases scattered throughout the Shantung Peninsula.

In August of 1914, the Japanese government forcefully suggested that the German military and merchant vessels remove themselves from Chinese and Japanese waters. With no word coming from the German commanders, the Japanese took that as a declaration of war and began to move their navy into a position to take Tsingtao immediately. The British, for their part, would help the Japanese by bolstering their already significant naval presence with two battalions of troops. By moving onto the German naval base at Tsingtao, they had lived up to their word and broken the neutrality of China.

Just a month after the Japanese troops landed and began their ground assault on the base in Tsingtao, the Germans surrendered. Though this may be the only major battle the Japanese took part in during the war, it was a significant contribution to the war effort.

With the German forces removed from China, Russia would be free to focus their attention on its western border, instead of having to fight on another front like the Germans.

Because of this defeat, the Japanese gained a foothold in China, a non-unified country, and were able to take control of not only the Shantung Peninsula but most of China, setting up this part of the world for decades of conflicts.

Zeppelin Raids

In 1900, Count Ferdinand Graf von Zeppelin came up with an idea for a new way to travel. This new mode of travel would be revolutionary and one that would come to be a tool used in Germany's war efforts to remove Britain from the equation. He had invented a giant flying ship that was filled with hydrogen to allow for flight and named it after himself, the Zeppelin.

It wouldn't take long for the German military to realize the advantage these vessels could lend them during wartime. After all, these vessels could travel 85 miles per hour and could haul about two tons of goods. The first test of this tool came over the skies of Antwerp and Paris. The missions in both cases showed great promise, and now the German leadership knew they had the means to get rid of the biggest thorn in their side, Britain. So, in January of 1915, the German government and military leadership moved their Zeppelin division in preparation for making their first move on to the mainland of England.

The giant ships were hard to hide, but the Germans knew that the payloads that they carried would deliver devastation no matter how much resistance they received from the British forces. So, the Zeppelins were deployed to the coastal cities of Yarmouth and Kings Lyn. The Germans hoped this would cause a panic and enhance the fear in England so much that they would pull their troops back to their shores and withdraw from the war. Attacking the coastal cities didn't seem to be doing the trick; the Germans knew where they had to attack. The hub of everything British would be the next big target. A little over four months after starting the initial Zeppelin raids, the mighty airships made their way to London.

On May 31, the Germans, guided by the lights of the Thames, moved one of their mighty Zeppelins through the skies over London. As the people of London drifted off to sleep, the German soldiers opened the trap door and began dropping their payload. The incendiary bombs and grenades silently plummeted through the pitch black, and seconds later, explosions rocked the city streets of the mighty British capital. The once darkened skies now lit up with the explosions and fires that rocked the sleeping city. Londoners were jostled or jumped from their beds; there were screams and shouts; the streets flooded with panicking people.

By the end of the first major raid on London, the Germans had dropped 890 bombs and 30 grenades. The attack was successful, and the Germans left triumphant, ready to use this tactic over and over again until the British relented. The success did not lie in the number of lives lost as they were light—seven dead, 35 wounded—rather in the fear and property damage that the English people had been subjected to on that fateful evening.

Zeppelin raids continued for the next few months using well-timed strikes to keep the British unnerved and on guard at all times. Eventually, the British would formulate ways to combat these flying death-dealers. The government instituted city-wide blackouts in the hopes that having no lights to guide them would hinder the Zeppelins' missions. Several significant sites and buildings were fitted with searchlights so that the Zeppelins could be spotted before they were able to attack. The police were also issued whistles that would act as air raid sirens to keep the sound of larger ones from being beacons for the Zeppelins to use to drop their devastation on the citizens of London.

These were mildly effective, but in 1916, the real game-changer made its appearance. Until that point, even though the British had planes (not many but some), none of them could fly high enough to reach the Zeppelins. To fix this problem, the British engineers had begun mounting guns on the newly manufactured planes. These guns shot bullets that could break through the Zeppelin balloon, which would ignite the hydrogen used for flight.

Though the British had unveiled this new very effective countermeasure, the Germans would continue trying this technique well into 1917, but finally realizing that the Zeppelins were no longer as effective as they were, they would move on to a new technique. This new method of attack would be more maneuverable and less noticeable; the Germans would begin using bombers to devastating effectiveness.

Churchill Steps Down

The Battle of Gallipoli led to the death of many Allied troops and did not yield the territory or strategic gain that was expected. The campaign was riddled with incompetent leadership and poor execution, both in the timing as well as the maneuvers.

Unfortunately, the weight of these failures fell squarely on one man's shoulder: Winston Churchill. Long before he was the British Bulldog and led his country to victory during WWII, Churchill had many enemies due to his more liberal and imperialist leanings. Because of his political ideology, stubbornness, and mishandling of the Gallipoli Campaign, he soon found himself demoted to a cabinet post that no one had even heard of before. After the Dardanelles debacle, the conservatives wanted him out of the admiralty, and they got their wish.

Churchill, feeling slighted and unfairly targeted as the person who had let this opportunity slip through the hands of the British forces, resigned from office. Instead of standing in the parliament, he opted to join the rest of the British troops on the front line.

He gained a commission into the British Expeditionary Forces and ended up in France. Serving with the Royal Scots Fusiliers, Churchill would have many close calls and eventually make his way back home in 1917. With his return, he set his eye on a political resurrection. The liberal politician would serve the war effort in a wholly different manner as he was appointed to be the Minister of Munitions in a very progressive government headed by Prime Minister David

Lloyd George. Here, he would work his way up and eventually be elected Prime Minister of Britain in 1940.

Conclusion

Sensing the end was near, U.S. President Woodrow Wilson stood before Congress early in 1918 and laid out his vision of what the post-war world would entail. This vision was comprised of 14 points aimed at maintaining peace in Europe and the rest of the world. Wilson predicted a victory for the Allies and said it would be up to them to set the terms of peace but do so with unselfish aims and greedy machinations. Things like international waters, restoration of occupied land, and the ability of nations to self-govern themselves all found a home in the 14 points of Wilson's speech.

By the fall of 1918, both sides showed the signs of the long and arduous four years of war. The Central Powers had taken a beating with major offensives like the Hundred Day Offensive. The rise of disease, starvation, and the conflict itself had wiped out much of both armies. However, the Allied

Forces had more ability to bring fresh troops to the front, and this meant that the Germans were severely outnumbered. One by one, the allies of the Central Powers began to fall to the Allied Forces, and as each fell, it became more and more evident that the war was coming to an end.

In October, both members of the Central Powers asked the U.S. president to begin talks for a truce. Both nations had heard Wilson's address to the U.S. Congress at the beginning of the year and felt that the points he relayed were fair. In fact, the armistice and subsequent treaty would contain a majority of the ideas expressed by Wilson.

On November 3, the Austro-Hungarian Empire would be dealt a crushing defeat at Trieste, and here, they would sign their armistice, bringing the war on the eastern front to an end. Four days later, in a railway carriage (which would play a role in the next Great War as well when Hitler took Paris) at Compiegne, the Germans and the Allies sat down to begin negotiations for their armistice. (Two days later, Kaiser Wilhelm II abdicated his throne and fled to the Netherlands.)

The German leaders came to the table, expecting a word-for-word document of President Wilson's plan, but instead, they met that, plus two significant stipulations added. They would not only have to pay reparations, but lands that had been gained plus some would be returned or ceded to the nations affected by the war. All the points discussed at this meeting would find their way to the Treaty of Versailles, the final ruling on the matter, and the peace accord that would appease the Allied Forces.

With the outline for the treaty laid out, all parties would gather again for the final signing. The final signing would take place in Paris and be led by the leaders of the big four nations—the U.S., Britain, France, and Italy. At the Paris Peace Conference, the final figures and stipulations would be hammered out.

The defeated nations attended the summit. They had been the instigators and, therefore, much like criminals in a trial, had no say over their punishment. The terms decided by the four major nations of the Allied Forces were presented in front of both German and Austro-Hungarian representatives. Though the severity of the conditions impacted both countries, Germany was hit the hardest. Germany would lose territory and ten percent of its population through the committee's redrawing of the nation's borders in eastern and western Europe. (The Middle East would be affected as well. Here, the redrawing of boundaries would set the Middle East up for decades of perpetual conflict.) Since Germany had been deemed the aggressor, they were solely responsible for all the reparations. In the end, this war ended up costing the German state and people roughly 33 million U.S. Dollars, which was to be repaid over the coming decades.

The severity of the terms was determined to be the only way to make sure that Germany would never be a threat again to the people of Europe and the world (it would have the opposite effect).

To drive this point home, the agreement also restricted the German military to only having 100,000 men and created a demilitarized zone in the Rhineland area of Western Germany.

German dignitaries protested against some of the new additions, saying that they were not part of the 14 points they had agreed to when beginning the peace talks. However, in the end, all the additional rules and terms were reluctantly accepted. With the final draft completed, the parties once again met. This time at the Palace of Versailles and on June 28, 1919, the Treaty of Versailles was signed.

The signing of the treaty changed the world forever. From it, new nations formed, current countries were expanded, and the world governing body, the League of Nations, was created.

This precursor of the United Nations would be the international governing body for almost three decades until finally being replaced with a more impressive and effective organization. The league had some wins but also succumbed to the self-interest of the more wealthy and powerful nations more often than not.

The ramifications of the Great War would ripple throughout the world for decades to come. Many historians criticize the Treaty of Versailles for its roles in creating more tensions. Of all the ramifications of the treaty, many feel the one that had the most significant impact on the future was the harsh terms placed on Germany.

These terms would lead to economic hardship, unemployment, and, eventually, a recession. These consequences of the terms of the treaty would lead to the rise of a powerful and very dangerous nationalist leader, Adolf Hitler, who would lead Germany into another war on the global stage just a few decades later.

Trivia Questions & Answers

History Student

Why was Archduke Ferdinand assassinated?

Answer: Serbian nationalists that opposed the rule of the Austro-Hungarian Empire over Bosnia wanted freedom and control of their own country. So, on June 28, 1914, Gavrilo Princip fired the shots that would kill the archduke and his wife, beginning the first world war.

Where was the first major battle of World War I?

Answer: The first major battle of WWI took place at Marne and lasted from September 6-10, 1914. This site is located in the northwest of France, about 50 miles from Paris.

The war lasted a lot longer than the parties involved had anticipated, so that meant more men would have to join to

keep the forces stocked. How many people would enlist in total?

Answer: Over the four years that the battle raged, 65 million individuals from both sides would join the fight.

Both sides had their coalition names. On one side, you had the Central Powers, and on the other, you had the Allied Powers. Three countries that were part of the Allied Forces were also known under another name. What was that name?

Answer: The three-country unit was known as the Triple Entente.

Which countries were a part of the Triple Entente?

Answer: The UK, France, and Russia. (By the way, the Central Powers were also known as the Triple Alliance and consisted of Germany, Italy, and Austria-Hungary.)

The war would eventually be taken up by a majority of the powers of the world, but who declared war first?

Answer: After the assassination of the Austro-Hungarian heir in Sarajevo, the first declaration came from the Austro-Hungarian empire.

There were few places more dangerous in WWI than the area between the trenches. It was so deadly that troops came up with a name for it. What did the soldiers call that area?

Answer: The name didn't have to be smart, just accurate. Soldiers called it "No Man's Land."

As a result of the war ending, a mighty governing body formed to make sure a conflict of this magnitude wouldn't happen again. What was the name of this group?

Answer: After the Treaty of Versailles, a global ruling organization known as the League of Nations was formed. This governing body was invented to keep things like war from happening.

How long was the League of Nations active?

Answer: The League of Nations would be active from 1919 until 1946. At this point, it dissolved, and the UN filled its place in the world.

Many factors led the world to war, but these main political concepts played the most prominent roles. What were the three movements that helped bring the world to the precipice of war?

Answer: The three social and political movements were imperialism, militarism, and nationalism.

Once the Bolsheviks took charge in Russia, the leader of that party felt it was time to pull his troops back from the eastern front of the war. Which leader made this decision?

Answer: In 1917, Lenin began to pull the Russian troops back to the mother country as he looked to start building a communist nation and wanted to have all his people there to help him do it. There were remnants of the White Army that needed to be taken care of before the new government could be formed as well.

The truce stopped the fighting on what day in history?

Answer: The truce was the first step in ending the war and went into effect on November 11, 1918. It would be a couple of months before the actual treaty would be signed, but this was a good start in ending the bloodshed.

When talking about the causes of the war, many people use the acronym MAIN. What does it stand for?

Answer: It stands for militarism, alliances, imperialism, and nationalism.

What neutral country did Germany march through at the beginning of the war?

Answer: Germany's move was intended to be in France, but before they got to France, they had to march through Belgium. This country had been neutral, and once Germany began mobilizing through its land, Britain soon realized they would be needed in the effort to stop Germany's aggression.

Why did Germany decide to attack both France and Russia?

Answer: It was all about alliances. The Russians did not support Austria-Hungary's annexation of Serbia and instead backed the Serbian nationalists. After this decision, Russia became enemies with Austria-Hungary, who had a strong alliance with Germany. So, the minute the Russian troops moved to the border, Germany moved to help their ally out. Russia also had an agreement with France, and the German leadership knew that once Germany and Austria-Hungary moved on Russia, the French were obliged to send troops to help their comrades out. So as a stop-gap measure, the Germans sent troops to cut off the French's capability to send their troops. This led to Germany ending up fighting a two-front war.

Which country did Germany declare war on first, Russia or France?

Answer: Germany declared war on Russia first. On August 1, 1914, Germany would make the pronouncement that they would be going to war with Russia. Two days later, on August 3, 1914, they extended the same proclamation to France.

When did the British Expeditionary Force (BEF) land in France?

Answer: The BEF first set foot on French soil on August 7, 1914. Though smaller than the French Army, the British forces were better trained.

Turkey would join the war after it had already begun. When did they enter the war, and on what side?

Answer: Turkey and the Ottoman Empire had signed into a treaty in 1914, with Germany as the newly-formed German State that helped them greatly with their military building efforts. On October 29, 1914, Turkey would join the war efforts on the side of Germany. Turkey felt they had to help and that by joining in with the German efforts, they could potentially destabilize the control of the French and British in other Muslim countries.

The Battle of the Falkland Islands was a significant win for the British naval forces. What date did this battle occur?

Answer: The Battle of the Falkland Islands took place on December 8, 1914.

And how many German and British soldiers were lost at the Battle of the Falkland Islands?

Answer: This battle was a decisive victory, where the British only lost ten men, whereas the Germans lost 2,000 men.

The *Lusitania* was a passenger ship that was sunk and played a significant role in the U.S. joining the war. Where was it sunk?

Answer: On May 7, 1915, the *RMS Lusitania* was attacked by the German U-boat *U-28* off the southern coast of Ireland.

How many people were lost when the *Lusitania* sank?

Answer: When the ship sank, 1,198 passengers went down with it, 100 of those being citizens of America.

When and why did Kaiser Wilhelm II abdicate the German throne?

Answer: There was a wide swath of unrest spreading across the German state. With a naval mutiny having just been executed and that growing unrest, the political leaders of Germany were convinced to push for the abdication. So, on November 9, 1918, Kaiser Wilhelm II left the throne and fled to the Netherlands.

What was the name of the general of the French Sixth Army that led the troops to success at the First Battle of Marne?

Answer: General Michel-Joseph Maunoury led the Sixth Army Division. This wartime hero had been retired for several years when the French Army called him back to service. In August of 1914, the 67-year-old artillery officer would find his way back to the battlefield and lead the Sixth Army to victory in the First Battle of Marne.

After being driven back, where did the German Army retreat after the First Battle of Marne?

Answer: The battle pushed the German forces back to the northern edge of the Aisne River.

The defeat at the Battle of Marne set into motion a series of flanking maneuvers on both sides. What were these maneuvers called?

Answer: "Race to the Sea." When the Germans retreated to the Aisne river, they began trying to use trenches to outflank their enemy. To counteract this, the other side started doing this themselves. This back and forth led to a series of trenches all linked together and protected at the top by barb wire, which was the real beginning of trench warfare during WWI.

What was the German Army's big mistake at the Battle of Marne?

Answer: The leader of the German forces moved his troops in the wrong direction. This maneuver created a hole in the German defensive line and allowed the French and British to separate the forces, weakening their ability to fight effectively.

And who was the leader that made the mistake?

Answer: The breach in the German Army line came when General Alexander von Kluck moved his troops north instead of west.

What were some of the reasons for the German defeat at the First Battle of Marne?

Answer: There were many reasons that the German Army wasn't at full strength, starting with the movement of 11 different divisions away from the line looking to advance and take over Paris. These divisions dispersed to other areas like Belgium and East Prussia as reinforcement for the conflicts going on in these regions. The German Army had also marched 150 miles without stopping, and the troops were exhausted. While they marched, they also saw many battles, which led to fatigue. The French Army was also not taking any chances and had begun demolishing bridges and railways, so that would mean fewer supplies as well as further to travel for the Germans. The Germans underestimated the French, which was a severe tactical miscalculation.

When was the First Battle of Marne fought?

Answer: The battle began in northeastern France, just 30 miles from Paris on September 6, 1914. Within the six days of the First Battle of Marne, the world would see many casualties and introduce some innovations. The battle would come to an end on September 12, 1914.

How many ships and sailors participated in the historic naval Battle at Jutland?

Answer: Altogether, there were over 250 ships and 100,000 sailors involved in the epic military Battle at Jutland.

Where was the Battle of Jutland?

Answer: The Battle of Jutland was the most massive naval battle in history and took place off the North Sea coast of Denmark.

When did the Battle of Jutland start and end?

Answer: The battle began on May 31, 1916, and ended just one day later on June 1, 1916.

Who were the admirals on each side of the Battle of Jutland?

Answer: Admiral John Jellicoe commanded the British fleet that saw action in the Battle of Jutland. For the opposition, the German fleet was led by Admiral Reinhard Scheer.

When did the Battle of Verdun take place?

Answer: The first barrage of German artillery began on February 21, 1916. The battle would last for almost a year and finally came to its conclusion on December 18, 1916.

How many casualties were there on each side?

Answer: Though the numbers are not wholly accurate, the estimate of lives lost in the 11-month battle comes to 400,000 on the French side and 350,000 on the German side.

Who was the German general who lead the Spring Offensive?

Answer: The German mastermind behind the Spring Offensive was General Erich Ludendorff.

How significant was the battlefront of the Spring Offensive?

Answer: Ludendorff chose a large swath of land to execute his Spring Offensive. A total of approximately 50 miles of the western front's Allied defense line would be the German's last great push.

What were the two goals that General Ludendorff had for the Spring Offensive?

Answer: Ludendorff intended to use psychological warfare and tactics to eliminate the British part of the resistance army. To do this, the central part of the plan was to drive the German Army between the French and British troops. Then turn north to deal with the less experienced British Army, thereby eliminating the French reinforcements.

Who was the French commander at the Battle of Amiens?

Answer: The man who spearheaded the Battle of Amiens for the French was General Ferdinand Foch.

What nations played a role in the Battle of Amiens as part of the Fourth Army?

Answer: To bolster Rawlinson's Army, he added infantry divisions from Britain, Canada, Australia, and America.

The Gallipoli Campaign, like all other battles, has been called many things. What are two different names for this tragic Allied loss?

Answer: This campaign is also known as the Battle of Gallipoli and the Dardanelles Campaign.

What does ANZAC stand for?

Answer: One of the pivotal forces in the execution of the Gallipoli Campaign was the ANZACs. This force was the Australian and New Zealand Army Corps – ANZAC.

What was the main objective of the Gallipoli Campaign?

Answer: Gallipoli was undertaken after Grand Duke Nicholas asked for help. The British naval command had reason to execute a campaign they had wanted to do for years. Not only would they be helping their Russian allies, but they would also be able to control the sea route from Europe to Russia.

Why did the Russian Grand Duke Nicholas ask for help from Britain in 1915?

Answer: The Russians needed a way to end the involvement of the Turkish forces in the Caucus Mountain area so they would only have to fight foes on one side.

What were the two beachheads established by the Allied Forces on the Gallipoli Peninsula?

Answer: The beachhead established on the southern tip of the peninsula was called Helles. Though later it would be renamed in honor of the fallen ANZAC soldiers, ANZAC Cove. The second beachhead was on the Aegean, and it was called Gaba Tepe.

When was the evacuation of Gallipoli ordered?

Answer: The initial order to begin evacuation came down on December 7, 1915.

How long did the evacuation take to complete?

Answer: The last troops did not leave until January 9, 1916.

What were the results of the Battle of Megiddo for the Ottoman forces and Empire?

Answer: The Ottoman's loss at Megiddo sealed the fate of the 600-year reign of this mighty empire. They were forced to sign an armistice on October 30. In this armistice, they agreed to the partition of their empire, giving lands back to previously-conquered places. Though it would take a few years for the final dissolution of empire (it wouldn't be until 1923, until it officially ended) altogether, this indeed was the final blow.

Where and when did the "Red Baron" die?

Answer: The "Red Baron" had been given his fighting squadron and was engaging the enemy in April 1918. As he swooped low to follow an enemy plane, he was taken by surprise by a machine gunner on the ground. He would take a bullet and lose control of his plane, nose-diving into the ground and meeting his end.

Who was Edith Cavell?

Answer: Edith Cavell, a British nurse, formerly from the Norfolk area of England, became a hero to the Belgian Resistance. She helped Allied troops escape occupied-

Belgium through a path to the neutral Netherlands and back to England.

Where was the *Lusitania* bound for when it launched?

Answer: The *Lusitania* launched from Liverpool and was headed to New York.

What former president of the U.S. demanded retaliation after the sinking of the *Lusitania*?

Answer: Woodrow Wilson decided not to instigate any ill feelings with the German state when this happened, but former President Teddy Roosevelt felt this was not the right move and called for immediate retaliation for the American lives lost.

When was the first Zeppelin raid on London executed?

Answer: On May 31, 1915, the Germans used the Thames River and its lights to guide them toward their most significant target yet, London. The doors opened that night and dropped 90 incendiary bombs and 30 grenades onto the unsuspecting people of London.

History Buff

War is deadly, but there was another fatal enemy during the war. What caused a third of the military deaths during the war?

Answer: It wasn't bullets or tanks. No, the outbreak of the Spanish Influenza took its toll on the military men and women of the Great War. There were three primary outbreaks, two of which were during the war.

What well-known moniker did the German pilot, Manfred von Richthofen, go by?

Answer: The illustrious German pilot is better known as the Red Baron.

How many enemy planes did he shoot down?

Answer: In his flying career, he shot down a whopping 80 British and French planes.

Which general led the American Army on the western front?

Answer: General John "Black Jack" Pershing was the commander of the American Expeditionary Forces (AEF) that fought alongside the French and British troops to fend off the advancing German empire.

World War I was known by a few different names. What were the two main ones?

Answer: The war would be dubbed World War I, but it was also known as "The War to End All Wars" and "The Kaiser's War."

The U.S. tried to keep from entering the war, but eventually, they would see that they needed to help their allies. What was the date the U.S. finally joined the conflict?

Answer: At first, President Wilson stated that the U.S. would stay neutral in the conflict. However, Germany's announcement that they were going to use submarines without prejudice to keep merchant ship's from entering Britain became a problem. This decree would lead to the sinking of the *Lusitania*, which had 128 American citizens on board. On top of that, the "Zimmermann Telegram" was intercepted, and its content threatened U.S. borders. This telegraph insinuated that Germany would ally with Mexico. At that point, Wilson had no alternative, and he sent America to the war on April 6, 1917.

Russia fought a two-sided war while the war ensued. On their western border, they were crucial components in the World War, but in 1917, they also began to experience their internal conflict. What was this conflict?

Answer: In 1917, after two separate revolutions occurred, the people overthrew the aristocracy and put the Bolsheviks in power. With that, the USSR was born.

What caused the political upheaval in Russia?

Answer: The people of Russia had enough of their Tsars and their lavish lives. They starved and struggled while the Tsars kept making decisions that only impacted them.

Tanks played a role in combat for the first time during WWI. What was the prototype tank called?

Answer: In 1915, the UK's Landship Committee began building a weapon that was intended to turn the tides. Dubbed the *Little Willie*, after months of designing and manufacturing, the tank made its way to combat in August of that same year.

Germany's decision to attack two fronts was a controversial one. In what document was this plan outlined?

Answer: Germany intended to attack the French on one side and the Russians on the other. The Schlieffen Plan would lay this plan out in detail.

Trench warfare was new, so there was a cost unknown other than the artillery and gunfire. The soldiers in the trenches experienced many medical conditions. Name two different ailments they struggled with.

Answer: Two medical ailments have been given their name for their extensive proliferation during the Great War. The first and most common was the Trench Foot. This condition was caused by long periods of exposure to dampness, cold, and unsanitary conditions. Many of the men were stuck in trenches, no matter the weather and without access to dry clothes. Because of this, they would end up with trench foot, which could lead to amputation in severe circumstances. The other ailment was known as Trench Mouth. This disease was a severe form of necrotic gingivitis. It was contracted by not having access to hygiene tools and exposure to unsanitary situations like the trenches of WWI.

The first battle of the eastern front was the Battle of Tannenberg. Why was it so important other than it is the first battle?

Answer: For the Central Powers, this battle showed the weakness of the Russian Army. This battle would lead Germany and its allies to be emboldened and put a little more effort into fighting on the eastern front. (Though most of the focus was still on the western front.)

After America joined the battle, there were a lot of open jobs. Because of this, a lot of African Americans moved to the north to fill these positions. What was this called?

Answer: Not long removed from the end of the civil war and still under the oppression of Jim Crow laws, the blacks of the south wanted to escape the systematic racism of the south. With the mass opening of jobs due to the war efforts, there was a need for workers, so the Great Migration began.

To have enough soldiers to send into battle, President Wilson and Congress enacted what act?

Answer: When the U.S. decided to help their allies out, they were not suited for conflict of this size, so they needed a way to get a ton of men into the service. On May 18, 1917, the Selective Service Act was passed. The law would give the president the power to draft non-disabled men into the military.

To keep the public from panicking and help prevent protests, the U.S. government passed an act that would make it illegal to criticize the government in publications or by individuals. What was the act called?

Answer: The act was called the Sedition Act.

When did the Sedition Act go into effect?

Answer: The bill was signed into law in April of 1917, just a few weeks after Wilson decreed war.

War is a pricey endeavor, and when America joined the cause, they did not have enough to fund the war. So what actions were taken to help with this problem?

Answer: To absorb some of the costs, the U.S. government instituted an income tax, war profits tax, and an excise tax. Along with the placement of taxes on this fund, the government also began selling government bonds.

Who was the commander of the Austro-Hungarian armies?

Answer: Franz Conrad von Hötzendorf led the Austro-Hungarian Armies.

What did Charles Whittlesey use to stop the friendly fire from bombarding his troop's position?

Answer: During the battle in the Argonne Forest, Whittlesey and his troops (which would later become known as the Lost Battalion) were trapped, surrounded by enemy forces. During the battle, his battalion would begin taking fire from the Allies, and he would use a carrier pigeon to send a message, letting the Allies know that their artillery was falling on comrades.

How many German soldiers did Alvin York and his unit capture?

Answer: During the famous battle of the Meuse-Argonne Offensive on October 8, 1918, Sergeant York and the men of the 82nd Division would capture 132 German soldiers.

What was the name of the U.S. aviation hero that was known by the nickname "The Balloon Buster"?

Answer: In a single week, Frank Luke took down 14 enemy aviators. Ten of those were surveillance balloons aimed at relaying tactical locations and troop movements to the German Army. For this amazing and heroic feat, the pilot was soon dubbed "The Balloon Buster."

The German aviation corps had the Red Baron, but what U.S. aviator had the most victories?

Answer: The most famous American flying ace of WWI was Second Lieutenant Eddie Rickenbacker. In his flying carrier, the pilot shot down 26 enemies, 22 planes, and four balloons.

How old was the youngest soldier to receive a Victoria Cross?

Answer: This honor would go to a young man who stuck to his post even after being fatally wounded. First Class Jahn Cromwell would receive this honor at the very young age of 16.

How many Victoria Crosses were awarded during and for actions taken in World War I?

Answer: Roughly 634 were awarded for bravery and acts of heroism in the face of extreme danger.

Everyone knows about the Red Baron, but there was another famous German flying ace that was a hero to his people. What was his name, and how many enemy planes did he shoot down?

Answer: The runner-up in the German aviation corps was Ernst Udet. This pilot would work throughout the war and shoot down a total of 61 enemy planes.

Just a year after the war began, Russia's ruler took control of the reigns of the army. When did he do this?

Answer: To reinvigorate his army, Tsar Nicholas II would take complete control over the Russian military on September 5, 1915.

To make sure that the BEF had enough recruits to fight the war, the government instituted conscription. When did this go into effect?

Answer: The British government activated the conscription ruling on January 27, 1916.

Getting your soldiers and weapons behind enemy objects is always a play when in the midst of war. Germans were able to get a U-Boat in U.S. waters during the war. What U-boat was this and when did it arrive in U.S. waters?

Answer: This was the first enemy vessel in U.S. waters since 1812. The German U-boat, *U-151*, entered the waters on the east coast with the mission of laying mines and cutting underwater telegraph lines. The submarine entered these waters on May 25, 1918.

After the First Battle of Marne, the war would be fought in the trenches, but that wasn't the only warfare that this conflict saw. There were two military tactics used that had never been used before: what were they?

Answer: Part of the reason the conflict at Marne was so successful was due to air surveillance, but this would not have been so effective without the radio intercepts. Airplanes were relatively new to combat, and being able to receive an audio transmission on troop movements leveled the playing field a bit a more. Along with radio intercepts, the use of the "Marne taxis" was the first use of the automotive transport of troops. Before this, it would have taken days for the soldiers to arrive to replenish the French Army. Going forward, these two military tactics would become the norm.

What advantages did the British fleet have over the German Navy?

Answer: The most significant advantage was the number of ships. In comparison to the German fleet, the British had 37 heavy vessels versus the Germans' 27 boats. For the smaller vessels, the British had 113 versus the Germans' 72. On top of the advantage of having more ships, they also cracked the German signal codes early, which allowed them to maneuver to counteract the Germans' tactical movements and brace for any potential attacks.

How did Vice Admiral Beatty lose three ships in the initial skirmishes of the Battle of Jutland?

Answer: These three battleships were not equipped with anti-flash protection. This flaw in their design meant that when shelled by the German fleet, the fire was able to make it into the powder houses. In turn, this caused massive explosions, damaging the ships enough that they would end up sinking or very damaged that they were useless to the naval efforts.

What time did the second phase of the Battle of Jutland start?

Answer: At 7:15 on the evening of May 31, the German fleet ran into the Grand Fleet.

What was the opening maneuver of the Battle of Jutland?

Answer: To form a blockade, the British ships wheeled to port 90 degrees. This maneuver prevented the German fleet from reaching their home port to recoup their losses.

How did the German fleet escape?

Answer: Admiral Scheer, knowing the battle and the fleet may well be lost if he couldn't retreat, had his ships do three separate 180-degree turns. This maneuver allowed the fleet to elude the tactics of their enemy and find a way to get back to Wilhelmshaven to recoup. In this battle, both sides took significant damage.

How many men and tons were lost in this battle?

Answer: The British lost approximately 6,784 men and 111,000 tons. In comparison, the Germans lost 3,050 men and 62,000 tons.

How did the Battle of Jutland change the German naval strategy during WWI?

Answer: The superiority of the British fleet was evident, so they course-corrected and began an attack on the British economy. This decision meant using their ships and U-Boats to attack commercial vessels.

Why did the German military strategists feel that Verdun was an excellent place to execute this attack?

Answer: The Germans were looking for a bastion of French pride, one that would drive the French to throw their soldiers onto the battle, no matter the cost. It also didn't hurt that the citadel was threatening the efficiency of the German communications line.

Who commanded a vital army division in the field and on the ground for the German forces?

Answer: Though the chief commander was General Erich von Falkenhayn, the ground soldiers of the Fifth Army were led by Crown Prince Wilhelm, who was the current Kaiser's eldest son.

How did the French come to be alerted to the German movement in the Verdun region?

Answer: In January, French reconnaissance planes noticed a strange surge of German troops along the area. However, it wasn't until February that French intelligence reported back to command of the forces amassing on the right bank of the Meuse River.

How long was the motorized supply train, and how many vehicles were in the convoy executed by the French for the Battle of Verdun?

Answer: The motorized supply train used for the first time in warfare to help the French stay supplied with both equipment and men drove down a 37-mile stretch of road. On this dirt road, about 3,000 trucks would travel, loaded down with the essentials to keep the front lines replenished and reinforced.

What was the road called?

Answer: The road would come to be known as the La Voie Sacrée or the Sacred Way.

Who was the leader of the French forces at Verdun?

Answer: At the beginning of the Battle of Verdun, the French High Command felt that there could be no better leader than the "Victor of Marne," General Joseph Jacques Césaire Joffre.

Who later replaced him, and why?

Answer: In May, after several defeats, the high command had lost faith in Joffre and decided to replace him with General Philippe Pétain.

How many shells did the Germans unleash at the initial artillery strike of the Battle of Verdun, and how long did it last?

Answer: The opening salvo of the Battle of Verdun took eight hours, and the German artillery launched approximately two million shells onto the French defensive line.

How many divisions did the German and Allies have at their disposal for the German Spring Offensive of 1918?

Answer: In preparation for the Spring Offensive, the Germans upped their presence on the western front. That left the German Army with 191 divisions available for combat during the Spring Offensive. For the Allies, they only had access to 178 divisions.

What was the code name given by Ludendorff to the first wave of the Spring Offensive?

Answer: The German code name for the opening skirmish of the Spring Offensive was Michael.

When was the opening salvo executed?

Answer: The Spring Offensive would launch on March 21, 1918, and would do so with a five-hour bombardment of the French defensive line.

How many mortars were used?

Answer: During this battle, 6,473 bullets would be fired as well as 3,532 mortars were lobed into that defensive line.

What two factors gave the Allies an advantage at the Battle of Amiens?

Answer: The advantages that made a huge difference were all types of deception. The first came backed by bogus communication. The Allies moved troops from the front lines to make it seem as though defenses were waning. In truth, the armies had been reinforced with nightly troop movements by other members of the Allied coalition. The Allies also used smoke screens as they began their push into German territory. The smoke gave them a tactical advantage over the weakened and demoralized German Army.

What hampered the success of the Gallipoli Campaign?

Answer: There was one main problem that kept the British forces from being successful in executing the Gallipoli Campaign. The first was a lack of intelligence on the people or the terrain. This lack of understanding of the ground, as well as the level of Turkish resistance, helped keep the British and their allies perpetually off-kilter as they went about executing their plans.

What two bodies of water connect via the Dardanelles?

Answer: The Dardanelles connected the Aegean Sea with the Marmara Sea.

Why was the strait important?

Answer: By taking this strait, it would have allowed the Allied Forces to safely transport supplies and troops through the strait to reinforce the Russian forces. This would help the Russian troops to stave off the advances of the Ottoman Empire.

Who was one of the British leaders who led the naval attack on the Dardanelles?

Answer: There were several leaders during this battle, but one of the top guys was First Lord of the British Admiralty, Winston Churchill. Churchill would bear the brunt of the fault for the unsuccessful campaign and would be demoted, eventually resigning altogether, and joining the front lines as a soldier. He, of course, would go on to become one of the most important men in the world and the leader of his nation during the next Great War.

After the first wave of attack, the naval battle was unsuccessful at Gallipoli; what happened?

Answer: After the initial failed naval attack, the British regrouped and planned a land attack instead that would be backed by naval vessels.

How many casualties were there on both sides during the Gallipoli Campaign?

Answer: Altogether, the casualties would tally about 500,000. Both sides experienced about 250,000 losses. Of those 250,000 casualties for the Allies, there were approximately 46,000 who lost their lives. On the Ottoman side, they experienced roughly 250,000 losses, of which 65,000 were deaths.

The Turkish resistance forces were led by a man that would later become a Turkish hero. What name does most of the world know Mustafa Kemal?

Answer: Mustafa Kemal was an imposing figure and one that had a deep sense of pride in his country. He would later go on to lead the way for the Turkish Republic after the Ottoman Empire was dissolved and would come to be known by the name Atatürk.

What happened to Churchill after the loss at Gallipoli?

Answer: He was initially demoted to an obscure cabinet position. Feeling slighted and a little by the fact that he was the scapegoat, he resigned and fought on the front lines with the Royal Scot Fusiliers. He would return to politics in 1917, and become the Minister of Munitions, and the rest of his career is, as they say, history.

There were a lot of transitions after the Battle for the Gallipoli Peninsula failed, even the British Prime Minister. Who took over after H.H. Asquith resigned his post?

Answer: A liberal government took hold after Asquith resigned and was led by David Lloyd George.

What was the Turkish name of the Gallipoli Campaign?

Answer: The Turkish call the campaign the Battle of Çanakkale.

What was one of the reasons that the Ottoman Empire joined the war?

Answer: Besides the fact they had an alliance with Germany, the Ottomans also thought that when the Central Powers won, they would regain control over the land they had previously ruled over. Places like Egypt and the Balkans were top of their list.

What two battles made up the Battle of Megiddo?

Answer: The two battles were the Battle of Sharon and the Battle of Nablus.

When was the Battle of Sharon?

Answer: On September 19, 1918, the initial battle of what would come to be called the Battle of Megiddo started.

When was Baron Richthofen (the Red Baron) born, and where?

Answer: Baron Manfred von Richthofen, the man known as the Red Baron, was born May 2, 1892, in Prussia—to be exact, what is now known as Breslau, Germany.

Baron Richthofen was born into a high-class family, and military service was expected. How old was Richthofen when he enrolled in military school?

Answer: Young Richthofen spent his early youth hunting and playing sports, but when he turned 11, that all came to a stop as he began his career path to military success.

When was the "Red Baron's" first victory logged?

Answer: The flying ace's first victory was on September 17, 1916.

Where was it, and who did he shoot down?

Answer: It was over France. There was a battle; he was able to shoot down a British fighter.

What medal did Richthofen earn when he collected his first 16 victories?

Answer: The medal was known as the Blue Max by the public, but its official name was the Pour le Mérite.

What was the name of the squadron that Richthofen was given command of?

Answer: Officially, the name of the unit was Jasta 11. However, because the pilots of this squadron painted their planes in bright colors and were able to do crazy aerial maneuvers, they became known as "The Flying Circus."

How many men did Cavell help get back to the safety of Allied territory?

Answer: The numbers are not definitive, but most reports say that she helped approximately 200 soldiers before being captured by the Germans.

When was Cavell arrested?

Answer: The Germans had kept a close eye on Cavell with spies and consistent inspections of her facility. Eventually, her extracurricular activities were detected, and in August of 1915, she was arrested and held for trial.

When was Cavell court-martialed?

Answer: She was arrested in August, but it wasn't until October 2 that she was court-martialed, and just two days later, she confessed with pride that she had helped those men escape.

When was she executed, and how?

Answer: She was found guilty of treason and was executed by firing squad on October 12, 1915.

Who was the first recipient of the Medal of Honor for heroism as a POW?

Answer: The first recipient was an executive officer from a naval vessel that was captured after his ship sank. Edouard Izac was captured and moved from two different POW camps while keeping the information he had learned on the submarine on his way to the POW camp to himself in the hope the information could help the Allies.

Edouard Izac had made several trans-Atlantic transport runs before a German U-boat sank his ship. How many trips had he made?

Answer: Izac had made four other voyages delivering supplies and troops to the western front.

How did Izac escape from the POW camp?

Answer: He waited for the right time, and under cover of darkness, he climbed a barb-wired fence and escaped into the forest surrounding the camp. He worked his way to the Rhine, surviving on raw fruits and vegetables. Once he arrived at the Rhine, he swam across to Switzerland and made his way to the Bureau of Navigation, which he reached on November 11, 1918, the day the war ended.

What other accomplishments did Izac go on to achieve?

Answer: Izac would end up representing California in the House of Representatives for California from 1937-1947. He was also a member of the House of Naval Affairs Commission. He was part of this when it inspected the concentration camps in 1945.

What were the 14 points that U.S. President Woodrow Wilson laid out to Congress?

Answer: When Woodrow Wilson stood in front of the Congress, his plan was to lay out a vision of what the post-war global community would be like. His 14 points included no secret treaties and alliances. He felt that politics should be transparent. The speech also stated that the seas should be neutral territory as well as all countries should be able to have free trade. It called for a global reduction of arms by every nation. The points also stated that Belgium should be reinstituted as neutral and independent once again.

Along with the territorial ideas, he also said that the Alsace-Lorraine should be retired to France and that Italy's borders should be drawn. Continuing with the boundaries and territorial questions, he also felt that the Balkan nations should be given independence and that those that were still under Turkish rule should be granted freedom. He also thought that the Kingdom of Poland should be given country status and more land. Lastly, these 14 points were the foundations for the League of Nations.

Who were the big four at the Paris Peace Conference?

Answer: The big four were the leaders of the big four nations in charge of overseeing the peace conference. This included:

Wilson from the U.S., George from Britain, Clemenceau from France, and Orlando from Italy.

Historian

The war wasn't exactly a world affair. What country was neutral during the war?

Answer: Norway was the only European country that remained neutral for the war. They even tried to do the same in the next world war, but the Third Reich had different plans and invaded them in 1940.

There were a lot of new things to warfare during this war. Other than trench warfare, what two other military weapons also saw their first action during the conflict?

Answer: The two pieces of equipment that would wreak havoc on the battlefields of World War I were the tank and the flame thrower. The British introduced the tank at the Battle of Somme. The flame thrower was a weapon produced by the Germans.

Over nine million soldiers died during the war. A good majority of these were under 30. Some were even younger. How old was the youngest soldier to see action?

Answer: Many young men rushed to their enlistment stations and lied about their ages to join. The youngest was a 12-year-old British boy. Sidney Lewis would put boots to ground for the first time at the Battle of Somme in 1916. Eventually, his mom would produce his birth certificate, and he would be recalled. He would later re-enlist in 1918 and spend time in Austria as part of the army of occupation.

Trench warfare was new to war and used very effectively on both sides of the western front. Because it worked so well, quite a lot of trenches were dug. How many miles of trenches were there by the end of the war?

Answer: Throughout the war, the soldiers of both the Central Powers and the Allied Forces dug 15,659 trenches. (That was almost 16,000 miles of trenches along the western front.)

One of the most critical military strategies apart from trench warfare was maneuver warfare. What is the definition of maneuver warfare?

Answer: This battle strategy was a very effective form of tactic and resulted in many victories. The basic principle of this strategy is tactics infuse the enemy through disrupting their maneuvers with rapid movement. These swift attacks and actions kept the enemy on their toes, and this increases the chance that they make a mistake.

Another form of warfare strategy was known as attrition warfare. What does this strategy entail?

Answer: This type of warfare entails wearing down the enemy through the use of tactics like blockades as well as constant bombardment. The intention, when using this style of combat, is to wear your opponent down both physically and emotionally until their will is broken and they can no longer fight. During WWI, this type of warfare happened between 1915-1917.

You have to have the support of the people, and the Prussian Prime Minister knew this. What did Otto von Bismarck use to convince German people in the south to support the war efforts?

Answer: Just 40 years before the outbreak of WWI, the Prussian empire locked horns with France. This is the war that brought a unified Germany and granted Germany control over the Alsace Lorraine. Using a new German pride and the threat of them losing land, he was able to garner support.

The Treaty of Versailles was vital in the revolution of the war, but one country rejected the treaty. Which country was this?

Answer: The United States opted to reject the treaty on the grounds that they wanted to stay out of European political affairs.

Though the war ended for everyone with the Treaty of Versailles, the Russians left the battle well before the armistice, and the famous treaty. What was the treaty that allowed Russia to end its war with Germany?

Answer: Lenin's decision to pull out of the war came to fruition with the signing of the Treaty of Brest-Litovsk on March 3, 1918. The name of the treaty came from the city it was signed in, which is what we know today as Belarus. With the signing of this treaty, Russia ceded to giving up over a million square miles of land. Germany and the Austro-Hungarian Empire would gain control over Lithuania, Poland, Latvia, and Estonia. The Ottoman Empire would gain Kars, Ardahan, and Batum. Whereas Ukraine, Georgia, and Finland would gain independence. Of course, when Germany lost, they were forced to give up the land they had accrued with this treaty.

The Second Battle of Ypres happened in 1915 in Belgium. The battle lasted a little over a month and was the site of two significant firsts. What were they?

Answer: The Second Battle of Ypres would see the first use of Canadian troops as well as the first use of gas by the Germans. The Germans would effectively use chlorine gas as a weapon to help them win the battle. The gas would be a vital tool for the Germans, and immediately after this attack, the Allied Forces began working on their gas. The Canadian First Division served at Ypres and lost significant casualties. This battle would also give a brave Canadian the honor of being the first member of the Canadian Army to win a Victoria Cross.

Airplanes were new to battle and needed a few adjustments to make them useful. One of these improvements was a unique propeller. What was this propeller called?

Answer: The propeller was called the "Systeme Morane." This propeller was designed with triangular wedges made out of steel and included to stop bullets from striking the propeller.

How big was the eastern front?

Answer: The eastern front encompassed 310 miles of land and stretched from Memel (which was in East Prussia but is now part of Lithuania) on the Baltic Sea to Czernowitz on the Romanian border.

How large was the Russian Army when the war began?

Answer: At the beginning of the conflict, the Russian Army held steady at one million soldiers. By the end of the war, the army had risen to over three million.

The Germans had the Schlieffen Plan, what was the Russian plan of attack called?

Answer: The Russians developed a plan of attack that would have them splitting their forces. In the north, the Russian Army would take two of its divisions and attack east Prussia, while three armies would strike Austria-Hungary. This plan was called Schedule 19.

The *Lusitania* may be the most famous passenger ship sunk by German U-boats, but it was not the first. What was the first passenger ship to be sunk?

Answer: On March 11, 1915, the German U-boat, *U-28*, sunk the British passenger ship *RMS Falaba*. The ship left Liverpool bound for the western African coast. Off the smalls of the St. George Channel, the German U-boat attacked and fired on the boat.

The war spread across the globe, even onto U.S. soil. A group of German sympathizers attacked a factory, blowing it up in Jersey City. What did the factory make?

Answer: To help their comrades across the Atlantic, a group of German sympathizers snuck in and planted bombs in the Black Tom Island Munitions Plant on July 30, 1916. This plant was making weapons and ammunition for U.S. troops that had just recently entered the war effort. They hoped to stop the flow of supplies to the Allied Forces. In the explosion, four people were confirmed dead, but that number may be up to seven.

The war ended with an armistice, not an actual surrender. There were two separate treaties, one for each front. When did each central power sign their armistices?

Answer: After the fall at Trieste, the Austro-Hungarian Empire signed the Armistice of Villa Giusti. This treaty was signed on November 3, 1918. On the western front, the armistice was signed on November 11, after the Battle of Redonthes at Le Francport.

What is another name for the Battle of Jutland?

Answer: The major naval battle is also known as the Battle of Skagerrak.

Who was the chief of the general staff and principal strategist for the German forces at Verdun?

Answer: Erich von Falkenhayn was a Prussian general of some note before he took charge of the forces at Verdun. He gained experience training the Chinese soldiers that would fight against the boxers in the rebellion. He was promoted to the Prussian Minister of War before replacing General Helmuth von Moltke as the chief of the general of staff in 1914.

What was Falkenhayn's edict for the Battle of Verdun?

Answer: Falkenhayn went into the Battle of Verdun with strategy and goals. These goals seemed extreme to some as he wanted a five-to-one kill ratio and to take the citadel at Verdun at all costs. His was a war of attrition, and he didn't care how much French or German blood was needed to be spilled to achieve his ultimate goal.

What happened to Falkenhayn after the failure of the Verdun Offensive?

Answer: The failure of the Verdun campaign haunted Falkenhayn for the rest of his life. After the significant defeat and loss of soldiers, the German High Command decided he needed to be dismissed.

Where did (and still do) the bones of the fallen soldiers end up after the Battle of Verdun?

Answer: When the battle was over, the dead found a home at Douaumont Ossuary. To this day, bones discovered are taken to the ossuary and laid to rest with the rest of their comrades.

After the initial offensive, how much land was covered?

Answer: After the first battle of the Spring Offensive, the Germans had gained 1,197 square miles of land and had taken 90,000 prisoners.

What was the second wave during the Spring Offensive's code name?

Answer: The second wave of Spring Offensive was executed on April 9, 1918, and was less successful than the initial foray. This troop movement was dubbed Operation Georgette.

What did the Battle of Amiens and the subsequent battles become known as?

Answer: The Battle of Amiens was the opening battle of what would later become called the "Hundred Days" Offensive. This push would be the final nail in the German Army's coffin and lead to the armistice.

How many lines of trenches did the Germans have at the Battle of Amiens?

Answer: The German defensive line was fortified by a sequence of three lines of trenches. These trenches, however, were poorly crafted with inefficiently placed wire along with the top and poorly-built dugouts.

What was the "Amiens Gun"?

Answer: The "Amiens Gun" was a German 280mm Krupp naval gun mounted to a railway carriage.

How many infantry divisions were in Rawlinson's Fourth Army?

Answer: Once Rawlinson's Fourth Army was beefed up, there was a total of 14 different infantry divisions along with several cavalry and tank units.

How many pieces of artillery, tanks, and aircraft played a part in the Battle of Amiens on the side of the Allied Forces?

Answer: On the Allied side, the Battle of Amiens was stacked. Not only did they have 14 infantry divisions but also a total of over 2,000 artillery guns, over 600 tanks, and 1,900 plus several aircraft.

How many divisions, guns, and aircraft did the German Second Army have at the Battle of Amiens?

Answer: In the corner of the German defenses, the Second Army was stocked with ten divisions, 530 guns, and 365 planes.

What was a "Whippet" tank?

Answer: The Allied Forces had a tank dubbed the "Whippet" tank. This tank was a lighter, faster tank that the Allies used for scouting missions.

What Russian Army was annihilated at the Battle of Tannenberg?

Answer: As the battle came to a close, the Second Army was led by Aleksander Samsonov. With no help from his fellow generals, Samsonov's men were outmaneuvered and found themselves running to the cover of the forests, but it was too late; the defeat was imminent.

The defeat at Tannenberg was cemented by the tactics and strategies of the German leader of the opposition army, the Eighth Army. Who was this leader?

Answer: Paul von Hindenburg led the Eighth Army. Hindenburg had retired but was recalled to duty after the war began. He led the Eighth Army in conjunction with Erich Ludendorff, who sat in the position of chief of staff. Hindenburg would go on to become president of the Weimar Republic and was also the man who named Adolf Hitler as the German chancellor. In contrast, Ludendorff would end his military career in defeat and go on to serve in parliament.

How many Russians died during the Battle of Tannenberg?

Answer: The losses of the Russian Second Army were significant, which gave the Central Powers a boost of confidence going into the following months. Fifty thousand men were killed or injured, and almost 100,000 men were taken as prisoners.

What happened to the leader of the Russian forces?

Answer: This type of defeat was not acceptable to Samsonov, the general in charge of this arm of the attack, so early on the morning of August 30, he walked unnoticed into the forest and ended his life.

Many battles in this war and others are known by different names. What is another name for the Battle of Tannenberg?

Answer: Because it took place near a town called Allenstein, it is also known as the Battle of Allenstein.

What was the date that the pivotal Battle of Tannenberg began?

Answer: The opening salvos of the battle began on August 26, and the battle waged for four long days before coming to an end on August 30. It was one of the very first and most famous battles of the first year of war and set the tone for quite a while to come.

After the war, the boundaries of countries were redrawn. If you wanted to visit Tannenberg today, where would it be located?

Answer: Tannenberg is no longer called Tannenberg. Today you would find this city on the map by looking for Stębark, Poland.

What advantages did Lieutenant Colonel Max Hoffman have that helped the German forces defeat the Russians at the Battle of Tannenberg?

Answer: Hoffman knew the Russian politicals amongst the generals. He obtained this information after Schlieffen sent him to observe the Russians during the Russo-Japanese war. Here, he learned that the two Russian generals executing the movements in this area, Rennenkampf and Samsonov, did not share the same views nor like each other. This dislike would leave communication, for which the Russian Army was known to be careless with anyway, few and far between.

Who was the general in charge of the XX Corps who fought against Samsonov?

Answer: General Friedrich von Schulz led the 20th Army Division of the Eighth Army at the Battle of Tannenberg. He would later become the commander of the Eighth Army when it moved east to fortify the lines at the Battle of Verdun.

Where was Samsonov's Second Army based out of?

Answer: The Second Russian Army had to march from their stationed base in Warsaw.

What limited General Rennenkampf's ability to advance and carry out his part of the Battle of Tannenberg?

Answer: Several factors hampered his troop's advancement. With the fortifications of Konigsberg and the Masurian Lakes, which made communication with Samsonov practically impossible, he only had a small 40-mile gap to move his troops through.

The Turkish forces needed help with their organization and asked for help from their ally, Germany. Who was the German general that helped lead the Turkish forces?

Answer: After being asked for help, the Kaiser could see no one better for the job of reorganizing the Turkish forces in Constantinople than Otto Liman von Sanders. The Russians saw this move as a threat and soon realized that they were right as the Turkish began to move in to help the Balkans and the Caucuses.

What was the first battle of the Brusilov Offensive?

Answer: The Brusilov Offensive would end up being a very successful campaign for the Russian forces. The campaign would begin on June 4, 1916, with the Battle of Lutsk.

What did the French ask their allies to do in February of 1916?

Answer: The French wanted to weaken the German forces, so they reached out to both the British and the Russians to ask them to plan significant attacks at different points. They believed this would split up the German forces and help them gain some ground. Both parties agreed, with the British beginning the planning of the Battle of Somme and the Russians looking to attack both Lake Narocz and Vilna.

What did General Brusilov push for?

Answer: Brusilov was a strategist, and knowing that the attack of Vilna was planned, he knew a way to ensure the defeat of the enemy soldiers. He reached out to the Russian command and pleaded with them to allow him to move his troops to attack in the southwest. He knew this would cause the enemy troops to be split up and, therefore, weaken the Vilna line allowing for victory.

The north may have been a campaign against the Germans on the eastern front, but in the south, it was all about the Austro-Hungarian forces. Who led these forces at the Battle of Lutsk?

Answer: The heir to the Habsburg throne, Archduke Joseph Ferdinand, led 200,000 men against Brusilov.

The forces that marched against the Hapsburg Prince numbered how many?

Answer: Brusilov was outmatched when it came to numbers as he only marched with 150,000. This difference would mean he had to be more strategic and use his years of experience, which is what he did and why the Offensive was so successful.

How long was the front that Brusilov wanted to attack?

Answer: Brusilov felt that if he were able to attack a line that went from the Pripet Marshes to Bucovina, he would be able to draw enough troops from the other front that it would give his comrades up north a good-sized advantage. That led him to attack a 200-mile front with just 2,000 guns. Along his push, he would capture over 20,000 prisoners before the Offensive came to a close.

After the first two days of the Offensive, how many casualties were there?

Answer: The battle was fierce for the first two days and left the field and field hospitals with approximately 130,000 casualties.

The success of the Brusilov Offensive led to what two events elsewhere in the war?

Answer: Because of the loss of forces by the Austro-Hungarian Army, the offensive on the Italian city of Trieste by General Franz Conrad von Hötzendorf had to be ceased so he could send reinforcements to the line. There were also four divisions of the German Army relocated from the front lines of the Battle of Verdun to reinforce the Austro-Hungarian forces further. The loss of this division can be directly linked to the German's defeat at Verdun.

When did the Brusilov Offensive end?

Answer: The offensive lost steam and officially came to an end on September 20, 1916. After pushing his way along that 200-mile front, Brusilov and the Russian forces gained 9,650 square miles of territory and cost their adversary quite a few soldiers.

How did Brusilov train his troops for the upcoming offensive?

Answer: The first and most important aspect of the plan was total secrecy. Except for Brusilov and his troops, no one knew what the plan was. Along with this, Brusilov used life-sized replicas of the places he planned on attacking. Starting with artillery, he made sure that the sighting of these guns was seen by air reconnaissance.

What was the Central Powers' objective at the Battle of Mărășești?

Answer: The Romanian forces had been causing some trouble, and to take Romania, they knew they had to defeat the forces. The plan was for the German Ninth Army and the Austro-Hungarian First Army to encircle the Romanian Second Army and wipe them out.

Who were the opposing forces at the Battle of Mărășești?

Answer: On one side, you had the Romanians and the Russians. The Russians had begun to feel the weight of events back home and would eventually leave the Romanians to fight. The other side of the line was a combination of troops from Germany and the Austro-Hungarian Empire.

Each side had many generals leading their respective armies and divisions. Who were the commanders on each side?

Answer: On the Central Powers side, the big names leading the two armies were August von Mackensen and Karl von Wenninger.

On the Romanian front, the two significant leaders were Alexandru Averescu and Eremia Grigorescu. Dmitry Shcherbachev led the Russian forces.

The battle was intense, and though the Romanians were outgunned, they still held the advancing enemy off. How many troops, guns, and heavy guns did each side have?

Answer: The Romanians started the battle with just over 200,000 soldiers, 280 guns, and 36 heavy guns. On the other side of the front, the Central Powers rolled in with almost 250,000 soldiers, 223 guns, and 122 heavy guns. Along with that, the Central Powers also brought with them 1,135 heavy machine guns, two armored vehicles, and 365 mortars.

How many troops were lost on both sides during the Battle of Mărășești?

Answer: Even though the Central Powers had the advantage militarily, the Romanians knew the land and used this for their benefit. Because of this, the Romanians had fewer casualties when the smoke cleared. They only lost 27,410 soldiers in comparison to the 47,000 on the other side.

What strongholds and cities did the Allied Forces take after the Battle of Sharon?

Answer: By the end, the Ottomans had lost Afulah, Beisan, and Jenin as well as the cities of Nazareth, Haifa, and Samakh.

What was the unit called that was a mixed division that captured the Jordan River crossing in the Battle of Nablus?

Answer: The unit was a division comprised of both infantry and mounted cavalry. The force was named after its commander Edward Chaytor and became known as Chaytor's Force.

What type of unit was Richthofen assigned to after graduating from military school?

Answer: Though he became known for his aerial superiority, he started his illustrious military career with the First Uhlan Cavalry Unit.

Why did Richthofen request reassignment to an air unit?

Answer: He had success in his cavalry unit at the beginning of the war, even winning an Iron Cross for his service. This unit had moved from the eastern front to the western front, where they were used for supply delivery. Feeling that this was not prestigious enough for him, he looked for a change.

What was the first flying squadron he was assigned to, and who commanded it?

Answer: Planes were new to war, and there was not a lot of units, but Richthofen found his way into one of the flying squadrons. His reassignment was to the Jasta 2, under the leadership of Oswald Boelcke.

What type of plane was the iconic Red Baron best known for flying?

Answer: The first plane he painted red and flew into battle was the Albatross D.111, but toward the end of the war, he upgraded to the Fokker Dr.1.

When the Baron crashed and died, he was behind enemy lines. What happened to his body?

Answer: Allied troops recovered his body. Knowing who this was and his service to his country, he was laid to rest with full military honors.

Like with so many things, this iconic aerial ace was not only known by his famous moniker. What other names was the "Red Baron" known as?

Answer: Richthofen was also known as le Petit Rouge, the Red Battle Flier, or the Red Knight.

What was the name of the school Edith Cavell helped find?

Answer: She left England and made a name for herself teaching nurses in Belgium and eventually helped open the Berkendael Institute.

What two countries fought for a reprieve for Cavell?

Answer: Both countries that fought for the commuting of her sentence were both neutral at the time, but they felt that the punishment was harsh, seeing as she was a medical professional. The two countries that fought for her were the U.S. and Spain.

Where is there a statue to commemorate Cavell's bravery?

Answer: There is a statue in her home country of England in London. The statue is located in St. Martin's Place.

What village was Aníbal Milhais' unit stationed in?

Answer: His Portuguese infantry unit was stationed in the city of La Couture.

What was the German name for the battle that Aníbal made his heroic stand?

Answer: It was one of the pushes during the Spring Offensive. This stage of the attack was dubbed Operation Georgette.

For his bravery, what medals did Aníbal earn?

Answer: He earned a medal from not only Portugal but also France. From his mother country, he received the Ordem Militar da Torre e Espada. From the French, he was also awarded the Légion d'honneur.

When did Aníbal Milhais die?

Answer: The Machin Gun Milhais lived to the ripe old age of 74, passing in 1970.

What profession was Ecaterina Teodoroiu studying before the war broke out?

Answer: Ecaterina had been studying at a girl's school in Bucharest to become a teacher before the war began, and then she volunteered to fight for her country.

What made Ecaterina decide to ask for a transfer from being a nurse to fighting on the front line?

Answer: There were two main factors in her decision. As she treated the men that made their way back to the hospital, she was a nurse and was inspired by their patriotism. Then her brother was killed in action, and she felt she needed to avenge his death.

What rank did Ecaterina end her career as?

Answer: She ended up leading a 25-man platoon as a Second Lieutenant.

Where did Ecaterina die?

Answer: Ecaterina fought at the Battle of Mărășești. During the battle, she was shot in the chest or head, the stories conflict. But it is said, however, her last words were, "Forward men, I'm still with you."

What was the name of another ocean liner sunk by a German U-boat not long after the *Lusitania*?

Answer: The *Lusitania* was one strike, but once the *SS Arabic* was sunk as well and the Zimmermann Telegram was intercepted, the U.S. was in a position where there was no other choice but to throw their support behind the Allied Forces of the French and British.

How many tons of war munitions was the *Lusitania* carrying when it went down?

Answer: Though at first, there was a denial of any munitions on board, eventually, it was exposed that the *Lusitania* carried approximately 173 tons of war munitions and supplies.

What pope suggested a temporary stay of combat to allow the troops to celebrate Christmas in 1914?

Answer: On December 7, 1914, Pope Benedict XV stated that he felt it would be a sign of good nature of the men to lay down arms to celebrate the birth of the Lord. It was not received well by the higher-ups of either side.

Which side initiated the Christmas Truce of 1914?

Answer: The night before Christmas, carols floated over the land known as No Man's Land, and in the early hours of Christmas Day, the Allied troops heard the faint tiding of

Merry Christmas. The Germans crossed No Man's Land without weapons to start a day of celebration.

What were some of the things exchanged between the soldiers as gifts?

Answer: There wasn't much to gift, but the soldiers used their ingenuity and gifted each other things like cigarettes and plum pudding.

What other more somber activity did some soldiers do during the truce?

Answer: Many fallen brethren's bodies had been stuck in No Man's Land that were unable to retrieve normally. So, to ensure their brothers had their way of having an honorable burial, some soldiers took this time to recover those bodies.

Why did the Japanese enter the war on the side of the Allied Forces?

Answer: Not only did they have an agreement with the British from 1902, but they wanted to begin expanding their power in the far east. This move was challenging to do with a German presence in China. So, they joined the Allied Forces to help but also to gain help in their expansion as well.

Why was the entrance of Japan into the war so pivotal?

Answer: Like the Germans, the Russians were faced with having to defend themselves on two fronts as the Germans had soldiers in Tsingtao in China. By Japan entering the war, not only were the Germans neutralized, but also having an ally on their eastern borders was helpful.

How many Zeppelin attacks in total were there on Britain?

Answer: There were fifty plus attacks executed on the nation of England.

What type of unit did Churchill serve in after he resigned his cabinet position in 1916?

Answer: Churchill picked up a gun and headed to the front to serve with the Royal Scots Fusiliers in France.

How much money was Germany tasked with reparations? When did they make the last payment?

Answer: The Germans were found to be the sole aggressor and were charged with paying reparations for the damages caused by the war. The bill came to 132 billion Reichsmarks or 33 billion U.S. Dollars. This large sum took decades to repay, and the final reparations for WWI were paid in September of 2010.

References

Krause, Johnathan (11 November 2015) Western Front. Retrieved from
https://encyclopedia.1914-1918-online.net/article/western_front

Dowling, Timothy C. (8 October 2014) Eastern Front. Retrieved from
https://encyclopedia.1914-1918-online.net/article/eastern_front

Murray, Nicholas (13 January 2016) Attrition Warfare. Retrieved from
https://encyclopedia.1914-1918-online.net/article/attrition_warfare/

Encyclopedia Britannica – https://www.britannica.com

History.com – https://www.history.com/

Kelly, Jeff (11 November 2015) *10 Forgotten American Heroes of WWI*.
Retrieved from https://www.toptenz.net/10-forgotten-american-heroes-of-wwi.php

Browne, Alex (3 August 2018) *10 Heroes of World War One*. Retrieved
from https://www.historyhit.com/heroes-of-world-war-one/

Andrews, Evan (31 August 2018) *6 American Heroes of WWI*. Retrieved
from https://www.history.com/news/6-american-heroes-of-wwi

Johnson, Ben, *World War 1 Chronology*. Retrieved from
https://www.historic-uk.com/HistoryUK/HistoryofBritain/World-War-1-Chronology/

bbc.com –
    http://www.bbc.co.uk/history/worldwars/wwone/battle_marne.sh
    tml

1914 – 1918 Online - https://encyclopedia.1914-1918-online.net/home/

Battle of Marasesti –
    https://www.worldwar2.ro/primulrazboi/?article=117

Battle of Marasesti –
    https://military.wikia.org/wiki/Battle_of_M%C4%83r%C4%83
    %C8%99e%C8%99ti

First World War: Battle of Megiddo –
    https://www.nam.ac.uk/explore/battle-megiddo

Kindy, Dave (July 2019) *Valor: Machine Gun Milhais*. Retrieved from
    https://www.historynet.com/valor-machine-gun-milhais.htm

Reed, Lawrence W. (4 December 2019) *The Courage of a Nurse: the
    story of Edith Cavell*. Retrieved from https://fee.org/articles/the-
    courage-of-a-nurse-the-story-of-edith-cavell/

HistoryNet – https://www.historynet.com/

Peoplepill.com – https://peoplepill.com/

Gannon, Paul (June 2014) *WWI: First World War Technology: Room 40
    Secret Intelligence Unit*. Retrieved from
    https://eandt.theiet.org/content/articles/2014/06/ww1-first-
    world-war-technology-room-40-secret-intelligence-unit/

Sass, Erik (August 2015) *Stalemate at Suvla Bay*. Retrieved from
    https://www.mentalfloss.com/article/67087/wwi-centennial-
    stalemate-suvla-bay

Acknowledgments

This is a special thanks to the following history lovers who have taken time out of their busy schedule to be part of the History Compacted Launch Team. Thank you all so much for all the feedback and support. Let's continue our journey to simplify the stories of history!

Steve Thomson, Wayne Lahr, Bill Anderson, Karol Pietka, David Ball, Patricia King, Charisse Peeler, Janel Iverson, Anita Midkiff, Nate Jones, Mike Blume, Pamela Mcnutt, Stephanie Shoulders, Dave Kaiser, Deborah Hughes, Adas, Joshua Sargent, Tom Daley, Axel Andersen, Christian Loucq, Joni K. Stewart, Jeffry A. Wheeler, Janalyn Prude Bergeron, Amanda Kliebert, Karin Scott, Lexi Nelsen, Robert Smith, Rita Masur Sweeney, Luc Hotte, Dwight Waller, Genifer Hall, Erica Jobe, Ellen M. Martin, Ellen Martin, R. Marc Vincent, Miriam Poe, Colleen Chiong, Farid Hedayati, Anthony Rodriguez, Christopher Tan, Ricky Burk, Arthur Goldsmith, Anne Mitcham, Barbara Wieczorek, Joan Bigham, Rick Conley, Mimi Hapsis, Holli-Marie Taylor, Charity Voskuil, Ray Workman, Judy Kirkbride

About History Compacted

Here in History Compacted, we see history as a large collection of stories. Each of these amazing stories of the past can help spark ideas for the future. However, history is often proceeded as boring and incomprehensible. That is why it is our mission to simplify the fascinating stories of history.

Follow History Compacted:

Website: www.historycompacted.com

Twitter: @HistoryCompact

Facebook: https://www.facebook.com/historycompacted/

Instagram: @history_compacted